dition, he discusses the disproportionate share of the earth's food capacity that is demanded by the more affluent countries with meat-centered diets.

Also provided is information on promising scientific discoveries in agriculture, along with 17 specific ways in which people can actively contribute to the solution of the world's food problem.

Here is a practical guide for all who are involved with agriculture and the food industry. It will also be essential reading for everyone who wants a clear understanding of what must be done to keep supermarket shelves well stocked.

ABOUT THE AUTHOR

Keith C. Barrons is an agricultural technologist with Dow Chemical Company, where he has worked in research and development for many years. Earlier he was a plant breeder with the Burpee Seed Company and in the agricultural faculties of Auburn University and Michigan State University. Listed in *American Men and Women of Science,* he is the author of more than 100 technical papers and patents related to vegetable crop breeding and chemical weed control. His accomplishments include discovery of dalapon, a grass control chemical now used internationally.

While on the MSU faculty, in a cooperative breeding program with the USDA he was co-developer of Great Lakes Lettuce, now the world's leading variety. Dr. Barrons, currently active on the Board of the Council for Agricultural Science and Technology, has served on a number of National Academy of Sciences committees, and also as president of the Agricultural Research Institute.

The Food in Your Future

Steps to Abundance

Harvesting corn for silage. The chopped whole corn plant will be discharged from the rear of the self-unloading wagon and stored in an upright silo of the type one sees on dairy farms or in a horizontal pit or bunker silo. With a U.S. average yield of about 13 tons per acre, corn silage converted to milk or beef is now one of our more important sources of food.

The Food in Your Future
Steps to Abundance

Keith C. Barrons

 VAN NOSTRAND REINHOLD COMPANY
NEW YORK   CINCINNATI   ATLANTA   DALLAS   SAN FRANCISCO
LONDON   TORONTO   MELBOURNE

To My Fellow
Agricultural Scientists
and Technologists

Van Nostrand Reinhold Company Regional Offices:
New York   Cincinnati   Chicago   Milbrae   Dallas

Van Nostrand Reinhold Company International Offices:
London   Toronto   Melbourne

Copyright ©1975 by Litton Educational Publishing, Inc.

Library of Congress Catalog Card Number: 75-22438
ISBN: 0-442-20587-2

Manufactured in the United States of America

Published by Van Nostrand Reinhold Company
450 West 33rd Street, New York, N.Y. 10001

Published simultaneously in Canada by Van Nostrand Reinhold Ltd.

15 14 13 12 11 10 9 8 7 6 5 4 3 2

Library of Congress Cataloging in Publication Data

Barrons, Keith Converse, 1911-
    The food in your future.

    Includes index.
      1. Food supply. 2. Agriculture—Economic aspects.
3. Food supply—United States. I. Title.
HD9000.5.B325   338.1'9   75-22438
ISBN 0-442-20587-2

Preface

Somewhere south of Milan on the Rome Express, my wife and I were seated in the dining car across from a woman from New York. As people from the same country on foreign soil are likely to do, we chatted over lunch about the delights and the problems of our host country. When I made some comment about Italy's large population in relation to land resources, she exclaimed, "I don't see why there's so much talk about too many people. Just look out the window. There's nothing; lots of space for more people to live in." She waved her hand at fields of green wheat in the fertile Poe Valley not yet at the heading stage. Incidentally, that crop turned out to be inadequate for the 55 million Italians. Only by importing grain were they assured of bread and pasta every day.

While thumbing through a magazine somewhere over the Atlantic en route home, I ran across an article by an environmentalist concerned with the broad subject of the quality of life. He shared everyone's desire for more parks and nature preserves and then went on to extoll our old methods of farming without fertilizer and with few crop and livestock protection chemicals. Obviously, he was quite unaware that today's farms produce twice as much food per acre as those of 40 years ago. What would be our quality of life if we did farm as he proposed? Even if every park and wildlife preserve and every bit of unused land was converted to food production, we would still go hungry.

Not long after returning to the United States, I overheard a tearful argument in a supermarket by a child who wanted his mother to buy some chocolate milk. Child: "Why can't we get some chocolate milk? You said I could have it." Mother: "There just isn't any left, darling. The store man says they aren't getting much because there's a shortage of chocolate." Child: "Then why doesn't he have a chocolate factory make some more?"

A woman on the train, a man writing for a magazine, a child in the supermarket; I hope their lack of comprehension of where food comes from and what it takes to feed the world's four billion people every day represents the extreme. Their expressions set me thinking about the food and agriculture facts of life that everyone should understand. I contemplated on how finely tuned is the system that keeps market shelves filled and how easily that system can be disrupted. I thought about those environmentalists who seem only interested in food and habitat for their favorite form of wildlife. Apparently, they do not recognize that People Food is part of the environment too.

I thought about the Hunger Mongers, those who unwittingly discourage the increased farm productivity needed by an ever-expanding population. I thought about the instances in which public policy has discouraged farmers from maximizing production. Is policy that can so profoundly affect the food in our future being set by people who have little comprehension of what modern agriculture is all about? Now, with the vast majority living in metropolitan areas far from the food supply system, do citizens and their legislative representatives have the understanding necessary to keep it in tune?

Here are my thoughts regarding the basic aspects of food and agriculture that I think everyone should comprehend. This is not a book about food problems in far off places nor about the threatened famines we read about in the press. You will find these problems discussed because they do have an impact on you, but this essay is essentially about *your food* with emphasis on what must be done to assure a continuing abundance.

I don't pretend to have all the answers, but my 40 years as an agricultural technologist have given me some insights into what it will take to keep a continuing supply of a wide variety of healthful foods on our supermarket shelves. I would like to share these with you in the hope that doing so will contribute to a wider understanding of how our number one need, enough food for everyone every day of the year can be satisfied. I will risk some predictions with which many will disagree. I am hopeful that this picture of agriculture in the 1970's will give you a better basis for your own crystal-ball view of the food in your future.

Keith C. Barrons

Acknowledgments

So many have contributed in one way or another that space will hardly permit mentioning all of them by name. I am particularly indebted to Paul Ludwig, Donald Spencer, William Seward, Al Wolf, John Monteleone, Delores Goulet, Gladis Klosterman and Kathi Waggoner for their indispensable help in manuscript preparation and review. My wife, Delphine, has been a patient sounding board on proposed subject matter and a constructive critic as writing progressed. Photographs were kindly supplied by the U. S. Department of Agriculture, Soil Conservation Service, Crops and Soil magazine, E. I. DuPont de Nemours and Company, The Dow Chemical Company, North Carolina Agricultural Extension Service, Plant Breeding Institute of Cambridge, England, and Auburn University Agricultural Experiment Station.

Contents

The Food in Your Future

Steps to Abundance

Hundreds of thousands of miles of windbreaks have been established in the great plains of Canada and the United States in recent decades. Here is a North Dakota farmstead made more pleasant through wind reduction and the presence of birds in the shelter belt of trees and shrubs. Crops benefit from long windbreaks such as those in the background.

1

You are Never Farther from Agriculture than Your Next Meal

Rapid changes in the world's economy since 1970 have left us gasping for breath and groping for an understanding of what has happened and why. Perhaps the change most difficult to fathom is the sudden shift in food supply from a prolonged period of surplus to one of shortage. Resulting price increases have hit everyone where it hurts most, in the pocketbook.

The petroleum crisis seemed easier to comprehend. There were the Arabs and their oil embargo together with more and more automobiles often giving less and less mileage. There was the shift to petroleum for heating and electricity. Meanwhile, we are told, new oil exploration faltered and there was the long delay in building the Alaskan pipeline.

But the food shortage seems less clear-cut. Some have tried to make it appear simple by referring to the Russian purchase of wheat from the United States in the summer of 1972. True, this came at a time when surpluses were on the way down, but selling grain abroad was nothing new for the United States. Farm exports have been a part of our lifeblood since colonial times. The Russian purchase of wheat in a year when their crop was short doesn't explain the recent tight supply of sugar, margarine and cooking oils.

In 1973 there was a shortage of meat, yet at this writing in early 1975 there is reported to be a glut in cattle feedlots and meat storage facilities. By the time you read this a new shortage may be on the horizon. Dairy products in short supply in 1973 were suddenly long in 1974, partly as a result of consumer resistance to higher prices. We read of famine in some part of the world one year and bumper crops with storage problems the next. After a quarter century of cheap and abundant food without ups and downs in supply to worry the shopper at the supermarket, it is little wonder that the confusing food events since 1972 have us concerned for the future. Remember how a few years ago we criticized the United States government for storing so much grain? Now some are equally critical of government's lack of a grain reserve program to tide us over lean years. With the rapid changes we have recently experienced, thoughtful people are naturally asking what the food supply situation will be in the future?

Food everyday! Food in enough variety for good nutrition and interesting meals! That has been the good fortune of most people of the Western World since we bound up the wounds of World War II. This hasn't always been true. Before looking into modern agriculture and considering the future, it is important to recognize that food problems have always been a part of man's existence. Only in very recent times, and then primarily in the industrialized world, has man been able to consistently have a superabundance of food without periodic shortages. It is difficult for us whose experiences span only a brief period of recent history to visualize the belt tightening and actual hunger most people throughout man's existence had to accept as a part of life. There have been great famines and some not so long ago. Forever impressed on the memories of elderly Irish immigrants I knew as a boy were the horrors of the great potato famine of the 1840's when a million people starved to death in Ireland and an equal number fled, mostly to the new world. Even now, prolonged drought is causing severe hunger in parts of India and Bangladesh. In a broad band south of the Sahara, prolonged lack of rain has forced millions of nomadic grazers to kill their herds, and many are facing starvation.

Now even we in the more fortunate parts of the world are having to look critically at our agriculture and food distribution system and ask: What went wrong? The weather? Just more people? A change in diet? More export demand? Farmers not continuing to improve their efficiency as they consistently did for a quarter century after World War II? I think it is some of each. There is no one cause and there is no one panacea. Farmers can vastly increase production if they have the right incentives, but let's face the fact that as population increases and export demands go up (as they will if the world enjoys a reasonable level of prosperity) the superabundance of the fifties and sixties with steady low prices will be but a fond memory. Most food must come from the land, and land resources are finite. They stopped making land some time ago. *You are never farther from agriculture than your next meal.*

Chances are good we are going to be facing food problems from now on. There need not be food crises but there certainly will be tough problems, ones requiring difficult decisions by national and international leadership. Individuals will have some decisions to make, too. Food problems of the future stand the best chance of solution if the public has an understanding of what is behind full shelves at the supermarket.

Perhaps current food price increases will contribute to this understanding. Perhaps a generation which thinks milk comes from paper cartons will learn what investment and labor and technology is behind a dairy farm and the processing and distribution system that brings its products to your food market or doorstep. Or what an intricate energy-demanding refrigeration and transport system is behind each head of lettuce once it is grown and harvested. Storage, preservation and distribution are just as important to your breakfast orange juice, eggs and bacon as the farmers who produced the raw food. The supplies he needs, the farm machinery, motor fuel, fertilizers and crop and livestock protection chemicals are all indispensable if he is to produce the stupendous quantities required to keep food on our tables 365 days of the year.

Perhaps current spot shortages will encourage us to give thought to the incentives needed to keep the system on target, a target of three meals a day for all. Perhaps the Hunger Mongers who unwittingly discourage progress toward increased agricultural productivity will comprehend what it will take to feed the world of the future. I am hopeful that all will recognize the contrast between man's finite ability to increase food production and his infinite capacity to increase in numbers.

Faulty nutrition does not always have an economic basis, i.e. a short supply or inability to pay for nourishing foods. Sometimes it is educational; many do not know what constitutes a healthful diet nor how to spend their food dollar wisely. Cultural factors often influence the choice of food to the detriment of dietary adequacy. But without abundance, a healthful diet may be out of reach of most pocketbooks. Without full shelves at the supermarket, nutrition education and cultural changes have little hope of reducing dietary deficiencies.

There are many technical and political factors that will have a profound influence on future abundance, on how well you and your children and particularly your grandchildren eat in the years ahead. To understand these factors, more knowledge of modern agriculture than possessed by the average citizen is essential. I hope the following chapters will give you some better insights into what policies you might influence that will give us the best chance of avoiding shortages. Can representatives of our vast urban majority, so far removed from the farm and the finely tuned system that transforms and transports farm produce to products on the supermarket shelf, make wise policy decisions at the national and international level?   Will they recognize that incentives adequate to encourage the investment of risk capital and hard work are necessary at all points in the system?   Will the public insist their governments avoid incentive-stifling overregulation of agriculture and the food industries?   Will citizens insist that the research and development and educational programs that have resulted in the doubling of farm yields during the past 30 years be given continuing support?   Will food production, processing and distribution receive priorities in times of a tight energy supply?   If all of these can be answered in the affirmative, adequate and healthful food for future generations should be assured.

An illustration of improved yield after supplementing a soil's mineral deficiencies. The corn on the left produced well according to old yield standards — that on the right gave over 100 bushels per acre. Without today's highly productive crops made possible by fertilization, vast acreages now devoted to pasture, forest and recreational areas would have to be devoted to crops for essential food production.

2

What it Takes to Keep Market Shelves Well Stocked

When we were largely a rural society with far fewer people than today, the bulk of our food was grown locally and distributed through channels that could not possibly cope with modern needs. Imagine the people of New York or London trying to rely on local farmers peddling their potatoes or milk, or on bread made from flour produced in a grist mill on the bank of a nearby stream. A highly intricate organization has become essential to the food supply of western societies in the mid-twentieth century. Here are the things that are needed to keep your supermarket shelves well-filled:

The land where most food originates.
The farmer with incentives for him to produce.
Favorable weather and adequate water.
Supplies the farmer needs from industry, including fertilizers, electricity and copious volumes of petroleum products.
Finance. You pay for your food at the check-out counter but remember that much of it was produced the year

before and at a high investment cost. There has to be a
banker.

Processing to simplify food preparation. What would you
do with a steer tethered in the backyard?

Storage to even out the supply. Could you handle your
fall-to-spring needs for potatoes if delivered the day
after harvest?

Transportation. A Florida cold-storage warehouse full of
frozen orange juice will not help you prepare tomorrow's
breakfast.

Distribution. Once the frozen juice arrives in your locality
it must move to retail outlets where you can purchase it.

It begins with land. Most food comes from the land. The three
percent of the world's food supply derived from the oceans or
fresh water, mostly as fish, is very important, especially in
countries like Japan and northern Europe where more seafood
is consumed in relation to the rest of the diet than in most of
the world. But no matter how optimistic one's projections for
an increase in wild fish catches or in controlled production,
aquatic foods are unlikely to grow in percentage much faster
than population. I wish this were not so, but to bank on vast
increases in food from the oceans and fresh waters is simply
not being realistic. Farming the oceans has interesting possibilities but the technical problems are horrendous and capital
requirements overwhelming.

The recently publicized culturing of microorganisms as a
means of producing protein also has possibilities but it is a long
way from making major contributions. Such methods indeed
have a chance of producing vast quantities of needed food and
research on this technology should be given more support. But
an organic substrate is needed for the yeast or fungus or bacteria
to live on from which they can synthesize protein. Pilot plants
using a petroleum fraction as a substrate are now in operation, but petroleum, as we have all learned recently, is not
a renewable resource and not available in unlimited supply.

Plant material such as molasses, a by-product of the sugar industry, or even agricultural wastes, can be used. I recently visited a yeast manufacturing plant in Taiwan where all the molasses produced by that island's sizable sugar industry was being "upgraded" to a 40 percent protein product useful for nutritionally enriching a range of oriental foods. But agricultural by-products still come from the land as would any primary plant product used as a substrate for microorganism protein production. I hope I am wrong, but as I see it anyone old enough to read this book is unlikely to see the day when protein from these sources will constitute a sizable proportion of the world's needs. *Let's face it, most food must come from the land.*

There must be a farmer. I suspect that most urban dwellers are half a century behind the times in their picture of the people who produce their food. Perhaps there are still a few country bumpkins around operating more or less self-sufficient farms, but they are not the ones producing the volume of meat, milk, grain, fruits, and vegetables and all those things that you expect to find every day, day after day, at your local market.

In times past there has been great emphasis on owning land, and the measure of a farmer's success was often how fast he paid off his mortgage. Nothing seemed so important as owning land free and clear. Today's crop and livestock producer is more concerned with the management of money whether it is his own or someone else's. Naturally he wants equity in his venture, but the large chunks of money needed for operations necessitates a willingness to work with other people's finances and the capability of managing them soundly.

He's still a man who loves the land and would rather farm than work at anything else if he can make a decent living doing so. The producer who really counts, the one who raises the volume of food that it takes to keep the nonfarm population well fed, is increasingly better educated and highly alert to new technology that may benefit his operation. His average age is greater than his industrial worker counterpart and it has been increasing. This is a trend that should be of concern to all of us who expect to eat well a decade hence. But with prospects of a better return for their efforts, the chances are good that more young men will be entering agricultural production as a field of endeavor.

The farmer of the 1970's is keenly aware of his importance to you, and he looks upon food production as an essential and noble enterprise. But he is determined to make a good living at it, one which gives a return on investment and labor as great as that in industry.

Weather and water.   The weather usually follows a pattern. Spring comes and it doesn't freeze in mid-summer even though late frosts can necessitate replanting or early ones in fall can cut a crop short. The weather tends to be dry in some areas so we provide irrigation when possible, while in others we do the best we can with the variable rainfall that most regions experience. Most agriculture is rain-fed and we must expect moisture extremes.

It is not only dry weather that a farmer dreads. One of the key factors in the sharp increase in food prices in 1973 was too much rain in mid-continent United States late in 1972 which hampered efficient harvesting. This was followed by floods in the Mississippi Valley in the spring of 1973 and many mid-western areas experienced serious planting delays because of excessive spring rains in 1974.

In both years considerable acreage was so inundated that some planting could not be carried out at all, while vast areas were planted late. More often than not yields are lower following late planting. The crop misses the best growing weather and is more likely to suffer if it turns dry in mid-summer. Then there is always a chance of an early frost as occurred in September of 1974.

But drought is the greatest farming hazard of all. At this writing, dry weather is causing extreme suffering in India and parts of Africa. Those past middle age well remember the extremely dry Dust Bowl years of the 1930's in North America. Only because we had reserves from the fat preceding years were we able to come through that lean period without food shortages.

Farmers have learned to do something about the weather chiefly by making the most of extremes in rainfall. Much land is tile-drained to divert excessive water so crops will grow and to permit planting and harvesting over a longer period. Irrigation systems are often built for areas where rainfall is inadequate, and where its distribution is undependable supplemental irrigation is provided for high-value crops. Minimum tillage to avoid soil compaction and restricted root growth as well as fertilization practices to encourage deep rooting are modern methods the farmer has of making the most of erratic rainfall.

In areas where rain is seldom adequate and irrigation not feasible, stubble mulch tillage is now in widespread use. Knife-like sweeps just below the soil surface cut off crop stubble and weeds, and then leave them on top of the ground to help reduce evaporation and wind erosion and to catch blowing snow. Whether the land is cropped annually or left fallow in alternate years to accumulate moisture, the stubble mulch tillage system developed by agricultural researchers in the old Dust Bowl Region of the United States is going a long way toward reducing wind erosion. Russia has recently adopted this tillage system for her newly developed semi-arid wheat lands east of the Caucasus.

But no matter what we do, extremes in rainfall will undoubtedly continue. Even when the total for a year is just about right, there will often be too much at one season and not enough at another. We will continue to have lean years and fat years as a result of weather and rainfall variations.

Behind the Farmer. I still have pangs of nostalgia for the kind of self-sufficient farm I knew as a boy. A few pieces of equipment, harnesses and fencing were about all that had to be purchased.

Draft horses and livestock were fed entirely from produce of the farm. But that kind of an operation was on the way out 50 years ago, and today it has been almost entirely replaced in the industrialized countries with a food production business highly dependent on manufactured equipment. Behind today's farmer is a long list of goods and services that he must procure in order to do his part in keeping the market shelves well stocked. The fact that his productivity per acre is twice what it was even 30 years ago is evidence that this new type of a farm is important to all of us. At the old yields, those obtained before hybrid seeds, fertilizers and modern crop and livestock protection, our current food picture would be bleak indeed.

Last year I visited an Indiana farmer who produces soybeans as a cash crop plus corn and pasture for a modest-sized cattle operation. Here is a list of his year's purchases:

A new silo.
Lumber for expanding and repairing his feedlot.
Fencing and posts for much needed replacements.
A complete tractor engine overhaul.
A self-unloading wagon for silage harvesting.
Dry fertilizer.
Anhydrous ammonia.
Lime for a portion of his farm.
Three kinds of herbicides.
An insecticide for corn rootworm control.
Insecticides for cattle lice and grub control.
New tires for a truck.
Gasoline and motor oil.
Hybrid corn seed.
Grass and clover seed.

The above list does not include a myriad of small items, such as tools, machine parts, etc. The bill for his improvements and supplies totaled $43,000. For every farmer today, there are at least two others producing the things he needs and two more storing and processing food and getting it to market. The whole chain is important, but an indispensable link is the manufactured goods the farmer must purchase if he is to maintain a high level of productivity.

The banker has a role. In 1912, my father, who had a burning desire to become a farmer, borrowed $1,000 from a relative, bought a team of horses and some used equipment and started farming on a rented 80 acres. All told, his equity and debts when he put his first seed in the ground probably did not total over $2,500. Dad's farming venture ended with the United States entry into World War I. Without this interruption he might have made it in spite of so little capital.

Today $2,500 would hardly buy a farmer's fertilizer need for a single year, not to mention seed, tractor fuel, herbicides and insecticides, interest, rent and equipment depreciation. Obviously, farmers do not use their own money for all these expenses any more than other businessmen rely on their own equity. Financing agriculture has become an important part of the activities of financial institutions. Without huge annual infusions of capital, we could not have the highly intensive and extensive agricultural enterprises existing today in the developed countries. One way or another, continuing the financing of agriculture on a large scale is essential to keeping the supermarket shelves filled.

Much financing of farm operations comes from banks but much is also derived from government backed organizations and from co-operatives such as the Production Credit Association in the United States. Processors and distributors of food are usually corporate in nature with conventional sources of finance available to them. The farmer in technically advanced countries, however, is usually a small businessman with special problems, i.e., high capitalization per worker and a long time span from initiating production until sale of his goods. He is assured that people will continue to demand food, but production risks are high chiefly because of weather variables. Society cannot afford the risks of decreasing food production because of inadequate finance. Continuing governmental participation when needed to insure high farm productivity seems imperative.

Processing adds zest to our diet.   How many foods do you buy at the market that are in essentially the same form they were when they left the farm? Milk, eggs, potatoes, fresh fruits and some vegetables and dry beans. That just about covers it. Rice has to be hulled and cereals made into flour; poultry and hogs and beef cattle slaughtered and prepared for market. Almost everything else we buy is milled or baked or canned or frozen.

It was not only primitive people that had an abundance during one season and a shortage in another. Commercial canning is only about 100 years old, and frozen foods and juice concentrates were almost unknown 40 years ago. Our forefathers often had to tighten their belts and they never dreamed of having a fresh salad every day in the year.

Just as transportation of fresh produce has made a great change in our eating habits, processed products have enabled us to have a wide range of foods regardless of season. Before canning, freezing and rapid transport of perishables, people ordinarily had to depend on things that could be dried, salted, or smoked or the meat animals that could be slaughtered as needed. There is certainly nothing wrong with dried fruits, and I personally think dried sweet corn provides a nice variation from the canned or frozen product, but it would get rather monotonous. Pickles and sauerkraut put down in crocks added to the diet of our forefathers, but several months of winter without a fresh, canned or frozen vegetable sounds pretty grim. There is no doubt that our food processing industries have helped provide better health as well as a more interesting variety of foods throughout the year.

Storage is essential.   Harvest of our staple foods and the feedstuffs that are converted to meat, eggs and milk generally comes but once a year. Without food and feed storage we would be no better off than the deer in northern forests which enjoy a super-abundance during the warmer months and suffer an acute shortage during the winter.

Our forefathers ate the deer, but with our present population the entire wild herd would hardly supply us with meat for two weeks. We can't hibernate like the bears and if everyone went south with the birds, Florida would burst at the seams. There is no choice but to follow the habits of squirrels and chipmunks and store enough until the following harvest.

Even that isn't enough. There are still those lean years to provide for as people have been doing for a long time:

There will come seven years of great plenty throughout the land of Egypt, but after them there will arise seven years of famine, and all the plenty will be forgotten in the land of Egypt; the famine will consume the land, and the plenty will be unknown in the land by reason of that famine which will follow, for it will be very grievous.

Let Pharaoh proceed to appoint overseers over the land, and take the fifth part of the produce of the land of Egypt during the seven plenteous years. And let them gather all the food of these good years that are coming, and lay up grain under the authority of Pharaoh for food in the cities, and let them keep it. That food shall be a reserve for the land against the seven years of famine which are to befall the land of Egypt, so that the land may not perish through the famine.

The seven years of plenty that prevailed in the land of Egypt came to an end; and the seven years of famine began to come, as Joseph had said. There was famine in all lands; but in all the land of Egypt there was bread.

From Genesis 41.

The modern storage so necessary to keeping markets stocked day after day throughout the year is far more than an empty building. Each commodity must be provided the special conditions it requires; an airtight seal for silage, continuous cold for frozen products and a special modified atmosphere for apples and pears. Stored grain for milling and for feed must be dry otherwise mold will take over. Protection against rats and other rodents is a must. And then there are the insects galore which love stored food. Chances are few readers remember the wormy raisins or maggot-infested flour and cereals that were so common even in the early part of this century before modern packaging and fumigation.

It was in the bulk storage that insects used to take such a horrible toll. Stored grain insects have been known since ancient times. Supplies placed in sealed tombs in ancient Egypt were found on opening centuries later to have been destroyed by some of the same species with which we are familiar. Early American colonists suffered great losses from grain insects, and the colonial army of the American Revolution at times had nothing but wormy flour on which to subsist.

Probably no type of pesticide has benefited so many people over so long a period with so few unanticipated or undesirable side effects as the grain and food protection materials widely employed in recent years.

Transportation and distribution are imperative. This morning I had my favorite breakfast at home in central Michigan, but only the sugar and cream on my cornflakes were at home with me. Chances are these two items were produced on farms not far away, but my coffee was from South America and my grapefruit from Texas. Although the cornflakes were manufactured only 150 miles away in Battle Creek, the corn the processor used had probably traveled across two or more states before being converted. The banana I sliced on my flakes was from Central America, and the jam for my toast carried a Pennsylvania label. The flour from which the bread I popped in the toaster was made no doubt came from the wheat belt of the Great Plains far to the west.

What did you have for lunch? A tossed salad perhaps; nine to one the lettuce was from California. And, if it's winter when you read this, the tomato was probably from Mexico. The hamburger might have been made from local beef, but if you ate at one of the fast-food establishments, chances are it came frozen all the way from Australia.

Try making a geography game of dinner this evening. I will gamble that you will be astonished at the miles traveled from the farm to your supermarket by the things you eat and drink. Tomato juice? Probably California, where a high percentage of our processed tomatoes are grown. Iced tea? South Asia, of course. Fish fillets? The North Atlantic is the most likely source. Potatoes? They might be local, but Idaho or Maine is a good bet. Canned corn? One of the Northern states. Celery? Florida or California unless it is in season from northern producers. Canned pineapple for dessert? It no doubt came from Hawaii or the Philippines.

It takes a lot of wheels and roads and ships and port facilities to keep the shelves filled and a lot of petroleum to keep our food moving every day from farm to processor to storage to distribution warehouse to the supermarket. As you push your basket down the aisles you are merely the final link in an intricate transportation and distribution network that begins at the world's farms and ends at your table.

Soybeans are now being double cropped in many long season areas by drilling seed directly in wheat stubble immediately after the grain is harvested. A special drill for planting in sod or stubble is shown above and the young bean crop growing in stubble is seen below. Weeds are controlled with selective herbicides.

3

Revolutions on The Farm

One often sees reference to our modern agricultural revolution, but the profound changes that I have seen in farming during my forty years as an agricultural technologist really constitute several revolutions. Together they have and will continue to affect food supply as profoundly as the original discovery of agriculture.

Intensive Mechanization

Chances are that if you were to guess at the identity of my multiple revolutions you would immediately think of the giant tractors and other farm machinery you see while driving through the country, and list farm mechanization as number one. Let's talk about mechanization first, even though I think it may come further down the list in relative importance. The internal combustion engine made it possible. Once this engine was invented, and with our abundant petroleum supply, it was inevitable that tractors would replace horses just on economic grounds. Horses eat every day and their food requires land for its production. Tractors guzzle

petroleum when in use but their costs in labor, capital and operation in relation to their contribution has been very favorable in
comparison with draft animals.

Fewer people were needed to work the farms because of
mechanization and this sparked a trek to the cities. As jobs
became available in urban areas the move to the cities intensified, thus creating a shortage of agricultural labor so the farmer
invested more in machines to make up for the labor he couldn't
hire. Farm mechanization "released" millions to work in industry, but an astonishing number of urbanites are really still in
agriculture producing the tractors and the motor fuel and fertilizer and all the other supplies that are so important to efficient
food production in the mechanized parts of the world.

Unlike improved varieties and fertilizer and crop protection,
a high level of mechanization is not indispensable to maximum
productivity per unit of land. Some countries like Japan, Egypt
and Taiwan are producing high yields with far less machinery
than used in North America and Europe. They mechanize when
necessary to increase productivity but use much labor for tasks
such as transplanting, weeding and harvesting.

The Yield Revolution

My grandfather took pride in his 40 to 50 bushels of corn per
acre and probably never gave a thought to doing better. After
all, his land was well manured before planting and he cultivated
twice and hoed once. When the European corn borer came in
he plowed under all old stalks early in the spring to keep the
moths from emerging and laying their eggs on leaves of the new
crop. What would he have thought of the 140-bushel fields I
saw being harvested last year?

The Yield Revolution has been keeping your market shelves
filled and prices much lower than they would otherwise have
been for the past three decades. Now it shows signs of taking
off in the less developed countries under the banner of the Green
Revolution. It is not dependent on a high level of mechanization.

Human labor can still do much work we now assign to machines. Let's look at a few yield figures for the United States:

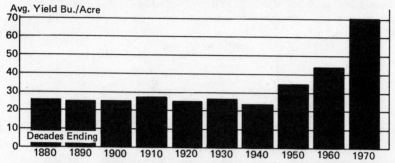

Figure 1. 100 years of U.S. corn (maize) production by decades.

Note the 100-year history of corn yields in Figure 1. The period of the 1960's showed an increase of more than 250 percent over the relatively constant yields of the seven decades prior to 1940. In spite of losses from Southern corn blight the 1970 yield of 71 bushels per acre was still more than twice the average of the decade of the 1940's. In 1972, the corn yield in the United States reached an all time high of 97 bushels per acre. After another good year in 1973, yields fell below 72 bushels in 1974 because of bad weather. Figure 2 presents 100-year yield trends in the United States for three cereals; wheat, oats and barley. Note the similar yield curves for these major crops.

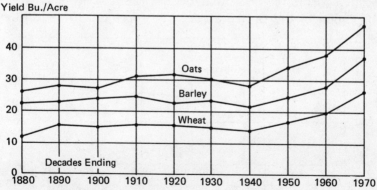

Figure 2. 100 years of U.S. small grain production by decades.

The following table indicates further how crop yields in the United States compare for two three-year periods 30 years apart and also for the more recent period of 1971-1973.

Crop	1938-40	Yield Per Acre 1968-70	1971-73
Corn	28.4 bu	78.0 bu	92.2 bu
Wheat	14.2 bu	30.0 bu	32.8 bu
Soybeans	19.2 bu	27.0 bu	27.7 bu
Sorghum (grain)	13.0 bu	52.9 bu	57.7 bu
Barley	23.0 bu	43.5 bu	43.2 bu
Rice	22.7 cwt	44.2 cwt	45.6 cwt
Corn (silage)	7.5 tons	11.9 tons	12.7 tons
Hay	1.3 tons	2.0 tons	2.1 tons
Cotton	0.5 bale	0.9 bale	1.0 bale
Sugar beets	12.5 tons	18.1 tons	20.6 tons
Beans (edible)	8.9 cwt	12.3 cwt	12.4 cwt
Potatoes	75.0 cwt	221.0 cwt	231.0 cwt
Peanuts	7.5 cwt	18.6 cwt	21.9 cwt

bu indicates bushels and cwt indicates hundredweight

Note the slower rate of yield gains in recent years with one slight decrease. Can further meaningful yield increases be realized in the United States? This question which is so important to the food in your future will be discussed in later chapters.

Figure 3 indicates the effect of increased yields during the recent agricultural revolution on the ratio of acres tilled to population in the United States. The downward trend in the

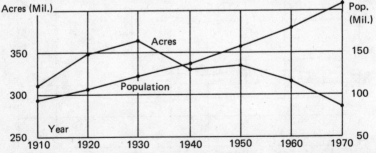

Figure 3.   Effect of increased yields on ratio of crop acreage harvested to population; United States, 1910-70.

area cultivated is not due to a shift in foreign trade. United States exports of agricultural commodities have increased more rapidly than imports over the past 30 years. Although there has been a reduction in the consumption of starchy foods, this change has been balanced by increased demand for meat and other livestock products, thus requiring more feed grains. The marked per capita reduction in area devoted to crops is largely a result of vastly increased yields per acre.

Extending Figure 3 beyond 1970, population has continued to grow although at a slower rate, while crop acreage has been stepped up largely as a result of recent increases in foreign demand. Assuming a reasonable level of prosperity with its resulting demand for meat, eggs and dairy products, it seems probable that crop acreage in the United States will remain well above the 300 million mark.

Comparable productivity enhancement has occurred with most crops in the technically advanced parts of the world. For example, potato yields in France increased from 97 to 208 one hundred kilo units per hectare over the last 30 years. In the 1930's Japan produced what were then among the world's highest rice yields, yet advances in production technology have resulted in a gain of approximately 50 percent during post-war years. The late Dr. J. V. Jacks, a British soils specialist, traced the yield of wheat in Britain since 1100 AD (Figure 4). Note the marked climb during recent decades after centuries of stagnation or slow increases.

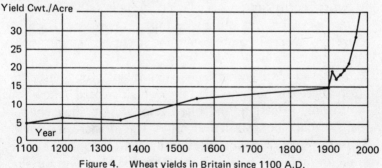

Figure 4.   Wheat yields in Britain since 1100 A.D.

What was responsible for the remarkable yield increases that have been achieved? With some crop species, a reduction in acreage with resulting retirement of less fertile land has in itself contributed to a gain in average per-acre yield, but this is by no means true of all. Grain sorghum, for example, was grown on an average of only 5.3 million acres in the United States during the years 1938-40 at a yield of 13 bushels per acre, while during the 1971-73 period 57.7 bushels per acre were obtained on 15.2 million acres. With most kinds of crops, yield increases are primarily the result of widespread application of advanced farming technology.

The past 30 years have seen the fulfillment of a century or more of dreams on the part of research workers striving for a more productive agriculture. Earlier progress was piecemeal. No sooner was one limiting production factor overcome than another took its place. In the past, improved varieties were often inadequately fertilized. Potentially good crops were severely damaged by insects or diseases. Then, about 30 years ago the results of research related to agriculture began to be put to work with a "systems" approach. Average yields started their sharp climb when growers eliminated multiple limiting factors. The technical influences involved may be considered in five major categories:

1. *Genetically Improved Varieties and Hybrids.* The importance of breeding has been emphasized in recent news about increased yields obtained with dwarf Mexican wheat, hybrid corn, and "miracle" rice. Actually, there is no successful agricultural enterprise today that has not benefited from advances in genetics and the scientific breeding of the last century.
2. *Improved Management.* Improved crop husbandry practices made possible through increased knowledge of soils, irrigation, and plant responses to their environment have contributed significantly to increased yields.
3. *Better Plant Nutrition.* Research over more than a century on the mineral nutrition of plants together with develop-

ments in the large scale production of fertilizers by the chemical industry made possible today's vastly better-nourished crops.

4. *Control of Damaging Pests.* The plant breeder has given us genetic resistance to many diseases, and research on crop management practices has pointed the way to mitigation of a number of pests. Many insects, mites, fungi, nematodes, and competitive weeds which so often reduced yields in earlier times are now kept in check by the use of crop protection chemicals.

5. *Farm Mechanization.* As discussed earlier, even in labor-rich areas certain kinds of equipment make it possible to irrigate extensively and to more adequately perform planting, harvesting and crop protection operations at the right time, thus increasing average yield.

In addition to production technology there are many economic, political and social factors that influence high yields. Credit must be available before needed inputs can be satisfied and a grower must have incentive to risk these inputs in the form of reasonable assurance of a market for his produce at a profit. This market assurance depends on storage and transportation facilities as well as on purchasing power and on policies related to price stabilization. Nothing discourages a grower from risking the costly inputs required for high yields more than the specter of low prices as a result of market gluts at harvest time.

Has the yield revolution run its course? Have we topped out? I do not think so, but there are many requirements that must be met to insure the further enhancement of productivity in advanced countries where so much progress has already been made. There is no doubt that the Green Revolution, which is but the first phase of a Yield Revolution in the less developed countries, has made a valuable contribution (what would their present food situation be without it?), but its future is full of ifs. All of the factors that have gone into the yield increase equation in the more advanced areas must be fulfilled. Will the developing countries have the improved seed, fertilizer and crop protection materials plus the social and political climate that encourages producers to innovate and take greater risks?

The Soil Fertility Revolution

From the beginning of agriculture until not so many decades ago man was a *destroyer of fertility*. He tended to overgraze, and when vegetation on his range and pasture was eaten too close to the ground the soil had no protection against erosion from heavy rains. Whole areas of the globe have thus been all but denuded. In the more level fields, crops were grown until the soil was exhausted of its available mineral nutrients and the farmer moved on. Terracing, practiced in some areas, was of much help but fertility often went down with continued use.

Then came the *conservation era in farming*. Rotation of crops with hay or pasture, planting of soil-building cover crops when land would otherwise be idle, integration with livestock with all the manure returned to the fields, control of grazing to minimize erosion; these are the tenets of conservation farming. It had its foundations in Europe two or more centuries ago and began to take hold elsewhere in more recent times.

Now, using conservation methods and supplying soil with the nutrients needed for optimum plant growth, man in many instances has become a *fertility builder*. During my 40 years of agricultural research and development, it has been my privilege to observe and at times to participate in the greatest revolution of them all, the fertility building revolution. Before that, we seemed doomed to deplete our soils or at best hold our own through conservation farming. We are now actually bringing soil fertility above its original level. In the process, our market shelves have been stocked with an abundance of food and can continue to be stocked if we wisely use the fertility-building technology available to us.

Here is how it works. First, a soil must be kept in place to maintain fertility. Wind and water erosion are still our greatest enemies. Once soil has run down the river or blown away there is no recovering it. North American agriculture's remarkable progress in reducing soil erosion, with its resulting pollution of air and water, stems in part from the conservation practices one sees while motoring through the countryside such as contour farming, strip cropping, terracing and grassed waterways. Not so obvious is the stubble mulching and other modified tillage practices in drier areas that have made a recurrence of the Dust Bowl of the 1930's most unlikely.

Although keeping soil where it belongs is an essential first step in fertility building, it cannot do the job alone. In addition to being kept in place, to be improved, soils must be supplied with essential mineral nutrients (often referred to as plant food) and also have physical properties suitable for crop growth. This physical side of fertility-building depends much on continually leaving the organic residues of vigorous crops in the soil. Both roots and the remains of top growth provide organic matter of great benefit to a soil's physical properties while improvement of its chemical make-up depends on the application of nutrients usually as fertilizer. Lime is often needed as a source of the essential nutrients, calcium and magnesium, and also for the correction of excessive acidity.

Heavy manuring will add appreciable organic matter and essential mineral elements, but to achieve good nutrient balance manure must often be supplemented with a phosphate fertilizer. Returning animal excrement to the land is ecologically sound and agronomically desirable, but manure is relatively unavailable in vast farming regions devoted largely to the production of crops, so we grow our organic matter for soil improvement through fertilization for high yields. In a sense, we grow our manure in place.

Fertilization with those mineral nutrients in which a soil is deficient gives it new life and leaves it in both an improved nutritional and physical state. Well nourished crops are big crops and the large amount of organic matter left behind after harvest, along with other sound management practices, truly make today's good farmer a fertility builder. University of Minnesota soil scientist, Curtis Overdahl, states, "Today's farming probably puts back twice as much organic residue as the farming of 30 to 40 years ago."

Too much soil is still not managed for fertility-building. Techniques necessarily must vary with kind of soil, rainfall pattern and climate. But we now have the knowledge and, in many parts of the world, the fertilizer needed to insure that all tillable land can be improved in productivity on a sustained basis. This is a goal that must be achieved if market shelves are to remain stocked with a wide variety of foods.

A New Era in Livestock and Poultry Production

If you are old enough to have motored through the country prior to World War II, you will no doubt recall a flock of chickens evident at almost every farm. All too often they had the run of the place, including the public road. I don't remember hitting one, but many a time I had to swerve my Model A so that a hen might continue her egg-laying mission in life. But where are the chickens now? We still consume lots of eggs and more poultry meat than ever before, yet one seldom sees evidence of chickens as he or she passes today's farms. In pens behind the barn perhaps? No, poultry are gone from the general farm. Both layers and birds grown for meat are now produced on specialized farms in tremendous numbers. Layers are held in cages and broilers in floor pens, but both types of fowl are highly confined, often with less than a square foot per bird. Feeding and watering is done automatically with special conveyor equipment and labor is kept at a minimum. These cost-cutting methods of raising poultry would have been impossible in the days of my Model A. Confinement rearing would have been disastrous because of disease. Losses were appreciable in the old days of the farm flock of a hundred or so birds, but with ten thousand in a single chicken house, diseases would have been catastrophic.

Confinement rearing of poultry and livestock with labor-saving methods of supplying feed and water together with vastly *improved disease and parasite control* constitute major changes in animal agriculture during postwar years. Coccidiosis control in poultry was a major breakthrough. This intestinal parasitic disease, now controlled by continuous medication of feed, always added appreciably to production costs even in days of the farm flock. Most internal parasites of cattle, sheep and hogs are now routinely controlled through medication and one costly pest, the cattle grub, is prevented from completing its life cycle merely by pouring a systemic antidote on the animal's back. External parasites have been conquered by better and safer insecticides while a range of veterinary drugs are available for most livestock diseases.

As important as progress in parasite and disease control has been to improvements in poultry and livestock production efficiency, it is certainly matched by *progress in breeding,* particularly with dairy cattle and poultry. Chicken and turkey are now considered relatively low cost meat but they were a luxury a few decades ago. You can thank today's remarkably fast growing breeds that convert feed to meat so efficiently. I recall an occasional outstanding milk cow among the herds in the vicinity of my boyhood home, but today they are practically all outstanding by the standards of earlier years. Dairymen have rigorously culled their herds in recent decades as a matter of economic necessity. Only the high producers could possibly net a profit and those giving a low milk yield would actually lose money. As a consequence, we have experienced a veritable revolution in dairy herd efficiency.

I am sure that some animal scientists would argue that these advances, confinement rearing, improved disease and parasite control, and breeding improvements, are all surpassed in importance by *progress in nutrition.* Each is important of course. One without the other cannot insure an efficient and profitable livestock, dairy or poultry operation.   But there is no doubt about the importance of our new knowledge of nutrition and its application by farmers generally.

Although I was an agronomy major in the College of Agriculture at the University of Minnesota in the early 1930's, I had classes in animal nutrition and biochemistry and I do not recall anything being said about the importance of amino acid balance to efficient hog and poultry feed conversion. Now we recognize the lack of methionine in many of the readily available poultry feed ingredients and supplement them with small amounts of synthetic methionine identical in chemical structure to the natural product. This nutritional advance alone has saved many dollars in your food bill over the last several years.

I don't recall hearing lysine mentioned in an animal nutrition class, yet today we know that corn tends to be deficient in this essential amino acid. Good hog feed must be balanced as to protein source, or alternatively, fortified with fermentation-produced lysine. Minor elements, so often needed by livestock whose forage or grain comes from certain deficient soils, were hardly mentioned. There just wasn't much known about the subject forty years ago. We learned about the importance of protein in the nutrition of the ruminant animals, cattle and sheep, but at that time the concept of using a nonprotein source of nitrogen, such as urea or biuret, so the rumen bacteria could synthesize the amino acids the animal needs was at most a gleam in the eyes of a few researchers. Now ruminant animals are receiving a significant part of their nitrogen requirements from less expensive sources resulting in measurable reductions in the cost of producing milk and meat.

Control of physiology through the use of hormones or growth promoters has added a fifth factor to the livestock and poultry revolution. One of the first widely adopted applications, the use of diethyl stilbestrol (DES) to improve the rate of gain and feed conversion efficiency in cattle is currently a controversial practice. Some data indicates that DES may induce cancer, yet there is no evidence that the mere traces which some researchers claim to have occasionally found in edible animal tissues are in any way carcinogenic. At this writing, the controversy remains to be settled. Other chemicals with a physiology-regulating action may make it possible to control sex, increase the incidence of multiple births in cattle and sheep and permit calving and lambing at a desired time. Still other substances that can improve rates of gain and feed conversion efficiency are on the horizon. I believe we are only on the threshold of a revolution in the control of animal and poultry physiology.

Like your dog with its flea collar, cattle now administer their own lice control with this back rubber. An approved insecticide is dispensed from a central reservoir. No longer is it necessary to spray cattle, thus risking chilling and insecticide escape into the environment. Cattle grubs are now controlled by merely pouring an insecticide emulsion along the animal's back.

4

Dollars-Yours and the Farmer's

You and I want to buy good food but we want it as cheap as possible, at the lowest feasible percentage of our income, since there are so many other interesting things to do with our money. We are all working hard hoping to earn more next year but we don't want to spend an undue part of our next raise on food.

Now let's do a little role playing. Say you are a corn and soybean farmer in the midwest who feeds some of his corn to hogs. You have equity of $25,000 in equipment on which you owe an additional $40,000. Some of it is showing signs of wear but a new corn harvester will have to wait until next year. There's a sizable mortgage on your home farm of 240 acres and you must shell out fifty dollars an acre rent on the remaining 200 where you are growing crops. It's February and getting late to commit for the tractor fuel, seed, fertilizer and herbicides that you will need as soon as spring breaks. After paying your tax bill in January your meager reserves are about gone and the family will have to live until a new crop comes in, or at least until you can sell some hogs in early summer. Your suppliers agree to some credit, but a trip to the bank is inescapable. A loan of $18,000 is negotiated to get the season rolling.

Will you be hoping and praying that present prices will hold if they are already good, or for an increase if they are currently low? You bet your last nickel you will! Especially when you look back at the years of 1969 through 1971 when you kept time as well as cost records, and in spite of all your risks and after the bills and taxes were paid you had only a little less than three dollars an hour for your time (and no overtime for the 16-hour days needed to get the crop planted in the spring).

Less than three dollars an hour in spite of all your risks and the business ability it takes to hold a farming operation together at all! Why, the janitor at the local school was making more than that without a single investment beyond the clothes he wore to work; no mortgage, no damaging floods or droughts, and no grueling hours at planting and harvest time. When we were snowbound last winter and almost everyone working in town stayed home, you had to move a lot of snow just to feed the hogs. You like farming, you are doing better than a lot of your neighbors and your prospects for improvement seem good. You're proud to contribute significantly to your fellow man's food supply, but you're damned if you think you should continue to get less return for your hard work than an ordinary laborer with little skill, no risks and no investment. You bet you're hoping for good prices on farm products.

You can play a similar role for the man slaughtering cattle at the packing plant or the lady working on the processing line where live chickens are converted to packaged broiler meat ready for you to pick up at the meat counter. Whether you're the owner of a farm supply store, an itinerant farm laborer, an operator in a flour mill, or a truckdriver moving produce from field to market, you're trying to do a better job and hoping that your efforts and the economy will make it possible for you to get a little larger cut. That's what makes the wheels go 'round and in the long run is responsible for our full supermarket shelves.

If you doubt it, let's take a look at Russia. She has tremendous agricultural resources but in 1972 had to buy large tonnages of grain from North America. Of course, her weather was not the best, but weather is only part of the story. Her farm people are all employed by the state and they just don't have the incentive. If it rains most all week but you can finally get in the field on Friday, where would we be if our farmers all quit at 5 o'clock Friday night and wouldn't go back to work until Monday morning? It may start raining again. We'd be out looking for grain to buy from some other country just as Russia has been doing. There can be no such thing as regular hours on the farm if the world is going to eat.

I once had an economics professor who introduced his course by saying that if we got the supply and demand facts of life through our head, we'd have 90% of all we needed to know about economics. Perhaps that was stretching it a bit, but it is astonishing to me how many people seem to ignore the law of supply and demand in their economic thinking (or is it in their lack of thinking). In any event, you can't repeal the law of supply and demand in dealing with farm and food economics anymore than you can with other commodities.

Food Is Not Automobiles

There is one point about food that is quite different from other commodities, namely, that most farm crops are produced on an annual cycle. Livestock and poultry may be raised on a continuous basis, but remember that animals and birds consume feed that is produced annually. When the supply is short for any reason it is going to continue to be short until the next crop is in. If there's a sudden increase in demand for automobiles, the manufacturer can step up production within a few months, but not so with basic farm commodities. Also, unlike automobiles, farm production can't be curtailed on short notice when a surplus appears on the horizon. Decisions on crop production goals must be made months before planting if a supply of seed, fertilizer and other needs is to be assured, and then the harvest comes months later. If you are raising citrus fruit or grapes or apples, you must order nursery stock a year before planting and then wait as much as four to six years for your first full harvest. It takes years and years to build a breeding herd of cattle. A basic food producer can't turn the production spigot on and off.

There is another obvious but often overlooked factor in food and farm economics that everyone should understand. You can get along for a while without that new automobile, or even a new dress or a new suit, and there's probably a little mileage left in those old shoes, but we all seem to have the habit of eating three times a day. If the food supply is even a little short, prices will go up rather rapidly because the demand is there day after day. On the other hand, people don't double the amount of food they eat if they have a little extra money the way they might double their expenditure for clothing.

If there is even a modest surplus of food, prices at the farm level are unlikely to rise more rapidly than the general level of inflation. At the same time, a modest surplus does not mean spectacular price reductions at the supermarket. The farmer may have to sell his produce for less, but this does not affect a major part of the cost of food that passes through the checkout counter. A reduction in prices paid the farmer has no effect at all on the costs of storage, processing, packaging, transportation and distribution.

Everyone old enough to read this book has lived through a period of agricultural surpluses and relatively low food prices. We were actually living in a fool's paradise when you consider the low return for his hours of labor the farmer received in the 1960's not to mention his investment and risks. This was pleasant for all of us who did not raise food for a living, but let's recognize that unless production continues at a high level, we can have no surpluses and indeed may have actual shortages.

A look back at post-war farm economics in North America will give us some insight as to why until recently we have had surpluses and relatively low food prices in comparison to the rest of the economy. Some historic perspective is necessary to an understanding of the present, and the present inevitably has a bearing on the future. Whether heavy reliance on mechanization came because labor left the farm, or labor migrated to the cities because their jobs were taken over by machines (I think it was some of both), the fact remains that the average North American farmer invested heavily in equipment during recent years. Expensive machines must be used if they are to pay off but the farm of twenty-five years ago just wasn't big enough to justify these expenditures. Those who could not or chose not to buy big equipment sold or rented their land to those who did. Today the average farm is about twice as large as at the end of World War II. Many if not most farmers recognized during years of surplus that prices on their produce would remain low if excess production continued, but the taxes and rent and payments on equipment came due regardless. The temptation was to farm all the land one could and increase yields with optimum inputs hoping to make a living through high volume. You benefited then through lower prices and you are benefiting now. If farmers hadn't had this drive toward efficiency, we would indeed be in a tight food spot at this time.

The log-jam of surpluses was finally broken by short crops in several areas coupled with greater protein consumption wherever the economy permitted, together, of course, with a relentless day-after-day increase in population. There may be surpluses again. I, for one, hope we can always have our granary filled with several month's supply as a hedge against lean years. But it is unlikely that we will again see a long period of surpluses such as we went through in the fifties and sixties. It could happen, of course, if there was a prolonged economic depression and people had to consume more products made directly from corn and wheat and other grains with a corresponding reduction in the conversion of these plant products to meat, milk and eggs. Remember, it takes several pounds of grain to produce a pound of food from livestock sources. If we reduced our animal product consumption significantly, there could again be sizable surpluses of grain. Actually we saw these economics at work in early 1975. The recession resulted in lower meat consumption and for a while the producer hardly recovered his costs. Consequently he fed less grain to animals and poultry so grain prices declined from the high levels of late 1974.

Food Prices Can't Always Be Low

What percentage of one's income should he or she have to expend for food? I would say just as little as possible, and I hope that agriculture can be so productive and so efficient that food prices will remain relatively low in terms of the average income. But there's no way they are going to be low all of the time and we have to expect periods of reduced productivity due to economic or weather factors.

Perhaps price controls are sometimes needed, but they are full of dynamite. If we are to avoid further sharp increases in prices when controls are lifted or, worse yet, a continuing short supply and an inevitable black market, controls must be managed in such a way that production is not stifled. Back to the law of supply and demand, if production goes down from political tampering, it will have the same effect as if production is off because of bad weather. If a grower's potential profits are reasonable, he'll continue to produce with some control of prices but not if he is going to lose money, at least not for long. If we have food price controls, they simply have to be flexible enough to keep production moving.

There's another very important factor in farm and food economics for the 1970's, one that didn't exist 20 years ago. In fact, it has never existed before to the extent that it does now. The United States is its own best customer for farm commodities, but not the only customer. During the last decade, much of the world has been experiencing increased prosperity with peaks in Europe and Japan, and much of this prosperous world cannot produce agricultural commodities as cheaply as we can in North America. Many countries do not have the technology or the land, and some have not applied the magic combination of hard work, capital, business acumen and land resources as we have been able to do.

When prices began to climb during the Korean War of the early 1950's there were price controls in the United States and they kept things in check until supply increased. But then we had fewer foreign customers bidding for our farm products. Most of the world was too broke to even dream of having chicken or roast beef for dinner. Now controls at the retail level will not insure a good supply of all the groceries you want. There are buyers in Tokyo for our pork and Germany for our dry beans ready to pay a higher price than controls might permit domestically. There seem to be customers in many parts of the world for our wheat and for our feed grains and soybean meal which they want to convert to meat, milk and eggs on their own farms.

Barring a worldwide depression, we are likely to see more rather than less foreign demand for our food products from abroad. When people have a little more money they are likely to eat better, particularly if in the past they have had meat only once or twice a week. Whether they import meat itself or feed grains to convert to animal products, it puts increased demand on the production of the few countries that can export significant quantities, Canada and the United States being among the leaders. Billions may still eat a lot of rice, the world's major source of carbohydrate, but if they have a little extra change in their pocket they're going to want bread once in a while, and that often means the importation of wheat. The North American housewife had better recognize that from here on she's got competition for the products of our farms. And, of course, devaluation of the dollar made our wheat, corn, soybeans and even our meat a real bargain in countries with a strong currency.

Export controls would be as full of dynamite as domestic price controls. Now that the world is so highly industrialized the products of our farms and forests are the things in greatest demand abroad. If we are to have the exchange with which to import the coffee you drink at breakfast and the petroleum you burn on the way to work, we had better create a social and political climate favorable to a very high level of agricultural productivity. Our economic well being as well as our food supply depend on it. Export controls to avoid actual shortages at home may sometimes be essential, but if the sale of farm commodities abroad is ever limited just to keep prices down we will be running grave risks of discouraging a high level of agricultural productivity. Even higher prices might then occur.

Meat Is A Luxury

During the time of rapid increases in meat prices in 1973, I heard a TV commentator say that "meat may become a luxury." Hasn't it always been a luxury? It takes five or more times the land, labor and capital to produce a given amount of meat as it does cereal products. This matter of meat versus grain will be discussed further in chapter 7. Meat is a luxury by sheer survival standards, although a healthful and enjoyable one which I think we should continue to have in moderation. Meat from ruminant animals can also have indirect environmental as well as economic benefits as will be discussed in chapter 5.

Our North American pioneers had cheap meat just for the shooting since the land on which the wild animals grazed was free. Later, cattle roamed the range and ate free grass or pastured on land for which a very nominal grazing fee was paid. Then came greater dependence on farm-reared animals, but still land was cheap, farm labor ill-paid, and in recent years grain for conversion to meat was the world's greatest bargain. As recently as 1971 a bushel of corn cost a hog raiser as little as $1.10, less than it was worth during World War I when $1 an hour was a top industrial wage. A portion of this low price reflected the lower production costs associated with higher yields but, nonetheless 1971 corn was the bargain of the century and this was reflected in lower prices to you for pork, chicken and dairy products.

The public outcry over increasing meat prices beginning in 1972 pointed up a profound lack of understanding of the economics of livestock production. My wife liked that 50-cent hamburger and those 80-cent roasts, too, but we were living in an unreal world. Let's look at some aspects of livestock farming that affect your pocketbook.

A livestock raiser or poultry or dairy farmer is a converter. Think of him as you would a local shirt factory. They don't make the cloth, they buy it and convert it to garments. Likewise, the farmer converts corn, grain sorghum, barley and soybean meal to animal products. Cattle, unlike hogs and poultry, can digest grass and hay. They get their start on these roughages, but the tender beef you demand comes from animals finished during their latter months on huge quantities of grain.

Now if the local shirt factory suddenly had to pay so much for cloth, thread and buttons that people resisted buying shirts at the inevitable new, higher price, what would happen? Or if the government set a retail ceiling on the price a store could charge for shirts and the factory couldn't make a profit, what would happen? They would close down, or at least curtail production drastically. A farmer who converts feed to milk, eggs or meat is no different than the shirt manufacturer except that he can't close down so fast. As a minimum he has the breeding animals to take care of (we would all soon become vegetarians if he sold these off), but he surely isn't going to increase production if trading dollars is all it will bring him, let alone a possible loss. Raising animals and poultry is hard work, one of the most demanding of enterprises. There are no weekends and no holidays from milking every 12 hours, and animals must eat and drink all the time.

Many farmers really have two businesses; raising feed and converting it to livestock products. It is just as if a big shirt maker also had his own textile mill where he made cloth. Now suppose he couldn't make a profit by converting his own cloth to shirts but he found buyers abroad who would pay him well for his cloth. To sell it to Russia or China for a profit instead of converting it to shirts in his own factory at a loss is not a tough decision to make. Now suppose you are an Iowa farmer raising 40 thousand bushels of corn a year and have a small feedlot where you fatten cattle. At times you have converted all of your corn to beef. Are you going to stick your neck out with a big loan from the bank to buy feeder calves and then take care of them all winter if chances are you would be just as well off if you sold your corn for cash at harvest time? You might even take that winter vacation in Florida your wife has been talking about for the last twenty years. If the Europeans want your corn, why not? They have to eat, too!

My wife and I recently lived in New Zealand for several months and nearly all the beef we had was strictly grass fed. In that country, grain has usually been more expensive than in North America and with cheap grass there was more profit in converting it to meat even though it took a little longer to raise an animal for slaughter. The beef was very flavorful although sometimes a bit tough. Now with high grain prices, more and more North American animals are being brought to market weight on grass as they always have been in most parts of the world. You will be getting leaner beef, good for hamburger and cuts that benefit from a tenderizer. It will be somewhat less costly than grain-finished beef, but it can't be cheap by old standards. The increased value of land and the high cost of fencing, fertilizer and haymaking or silage-making equipment rule that out. Nonetheless, if pastures are well managed, holding cattle longer on grass, possibly with a short finishing period on grain, cannot help but benefit your food budget through somewhat less costly meat and even more important, through a lowering of pressure on grain supplies.

Where Does Your Food Dollar Go?

The influence of the agricultural producer's return for his products on the price you pay at the supermarket has long been the subject of publicity and misconceptions. On the average, it is less than half the retail price and at this writing is only about 40 percent. All the people who process, store, transport and distribute food between the farm and the supermarket shelf must be paid and they are naturally striving to increase their income. An increase in spread between farm prices and retail prices tends to occur when the former dips because none of these other costs go down. Further, there is a lag in possible reductions in retail food prices, partly because the merchant may still be selling products he bought or contracted for before the farmers return was reduced! There is also the reluctance of a retailer to lower prices until competition dictates.

Averages can be misleading and the average part of your food dollar that goes to the farmer is no exception. His share is very low indeed for many prepared foods, such as fancy baked goods, TV dinners and the like. On the other hand, the farmer ordinarily gets an appreciable share on basic foods that require less processing such as flour, rice, beans, etc. Thus a lowering of the price the farmer receives should be reflected in a significant change in retail prices of such items but may have no discernable effect where, say, a small amount of flour, sugar and other ingredients is made into fancy baked goods.

I was struck by the cost of processing on a recent trip to the supermarket. Rice was on the shopping list my wife had given me and I found a good grade of short-grain rice in a three-pound package for $1.13, about 38¢ a pound. In the next aisle, I happened to see puffed rice in a large economy package marked 67¢ for 12 ounces, which figures out to about 88¢ a pound. If rice comes down from its relatively high price at this writing, I am sure the puffed variety will not be appreciably reduced. I have nothing against puffed rice, but don't get the idea the rice farmer is making an excessive profit because of its high cost. Certainly the grower had nothing to do with the puffing process. Rather a high price for air!

About half of the food distribution costs between the farm and your table go directly to labor. The rest is divided between transportation, packaging and other inputs. There are, no doubt, many untapped opportunities for savings in food distribution, but to have an appreciable impact on your food bill, labor-saving methods must figure high in any changes.

There is a temptation to confuse food costs with service costs and even the cost of nonfood items which are sold at the supermarket. Not long ago I heard an irate housewife just ahead of me in the checkout line berate the farmer and the government for high food prices. I noted her purchases as she removed them from her basket:

A carton of cigarettes
One large box of laundry soap
A package of paper towels
Four TV dinners
Two cartons of cookies
A carton of milk
One sack of flour

Obviously, the first three items have nothing to do with food economics. The TV dinners and cookies were food all right, but the money the farmer received for the raw materials that went into their preparation played a very minor role in their costs and final retail pricing. It is fine to have your meals prepared for you by a restaurant or a baker or other processor or, for that matter, by a domestic servant, but don't lay the cost of these services at the door of the farmer. He got only a few cents on the retail dollar spent on the prepared foods but fared better on the milk and the flour. You still had to pay for milling, pasteurization, packaging and distribution, but the modest spread between the farmer's share of these items and your final cost is a tribute to a highly efficient distribution system.

Is there any way to beat increased food costs? High agricultural productivity is absolutely essential to favorable prices for the consumer. Without it they inevitably go up even though with it they do not seem to go down as much as one would expect. Processing efficiency can vary and does have an impact, but storage and transportation charges are more or less fixed by equipment and facility costs, electricity, motor fuel charges and labor rates. At the retail level there are variations in efficiency, but large supermarket organizations are already doing a pretty good job often with a net profit of less than one percent of the sales dollar. Savings in food costs largely depend on the individual's willingness to rely more on the basics with home preparation and to avoid out-of-season produce or items that are temporarily in short supply. Shopping where prices are most favorable naturally can benefit the individual's food budget and also, if practiced by enough people, tends to bring prices in general down through competition. The food section in many papers gives tips on the best current "buys" based on U.S. Department of Agriculture production and pricing information. Most important is your willingness to follow the supermarket ads, to shop around and to buy larger sized units when they offer a genuine savings. Don't overlook the farm markets. Buying co-operatives can help, particularly when the individual contributes services and the organization is large enough to command favorable wholesale prices.

Political action and complaints about farmers getting rich or the "middleman" making an exorbitant profit is a tried but unsuccessful way to keep food prices down at the retail level. Under most conditions price controls are like an aspirin for a headache resulting from a deep-seated malady. As soon as they are lifted, the law of supply and demand begins to take over and the headache returns. Political action to insure the technology and incentives needed for high farm productivity with a minimum of disincentives would seem more effective.

Press and TV publicity about the farmers' occasional attempts to obtain a better price after their crop or livestock is actually grown has led to public misconception as to how much influence they have. Actually it is very little. Nonperishables may be temporarily withheld from market and occasionally perishables destroyed or left in the field. Producers negotiate for the best they can get when they are raising processing crops on advanced contract. But for the most part the farmer takes what the market offers. He can't very well calculate his costs, add on his expected profit and then publish his selling price. There are just too many farmers to permit doing this, particularly when their crops or livestock have already been raised and are in inventory.

Except in rare instances with specialty crops, it's not the producer who sets the price but the wholesale buyer or processor who is trying to procure his share of the supply. If it is on the scarce side, the inevitable happens and prices strengthen. Commodity traders dealing in futures also have an influence, but except in occasional instances of market rigging they also respond to economic laws, in their case, anticipated future supply and future demand.

Should We Insure A Grain Reserve?

The agricultural news tends to emphasize disasters. Perhaps there is little news value in a good crop growing the way we hope it always will. But a flood, a drought or an epidemic of a livestock or plant disease often makes headlines. People really interested in the status of agricultural production have many sources of information. In the United States the monthly publication, *Crop Production,* is available from the Statistical Reporting Service, U.S. Department of Agriculture, Washington, D.C. World-wide news related to agriculture is available in the U.S. Department of Agriculture weekly publication, *Foreign Agriculture,* available by subscription from the Superintendent of Documents, Government Printing Office, Washington, D.C.

It is important to recognize that forecasts have to be made based on current conditions and the expectation of average conditions prevailing as the crop progresses. But an average is by its very definition made up of extremes. Occasionally things turn out better than the forecasts predict but more often they seem to go the other way. Lack of rainfall at a critical period, particularly if subsoil moisture reserves are low, can be disastrous. While working at the Alabama Agricultural Experiment Station years ago, I observed the results of a colleague's irrigation experiments with snap beans. One year early growth was remarkably fine and the large bushy plants were in full flower when soil moisture dropped to a level where water was needed. No rain came. The plots receiving one inch of supplemental irrigation produced over three tons of high quality green snap beans per acre while the nonirrigated plot produced less than one ton and many of the pods were small and poorly shaped. Imagine the equivalent of an inch of rain at a critical time making a difference in yield of over threefold!

This sort of thing actually happens out in the real world of farming and it is just about what happened to wheat in Russia in 1972. Subsoil moisture was low and good rainfall distribution was needed for a decent crop. When rains did not come in late June and the first week of July, the Russian authorities knew they had to buy grain or ask 200 million people to tighten their belts. Their purchasing agents descended on United States grain merchants and acquired their needs quickly before this increased demand had a chance to be reflected in higher prices.

These large purchases which no doubt accelerated food price increases already on the horizon have been a matter of much "after-the-fact" public concern. Had congressional and agricultural leadership been more alert, the export subsidy, continued from the days when surplus grain was a major government headache, would not have been granted the merchants. Perhaps a requirement that foreign purchasing intentions be made known in advance of negotiations would have resulted in a higher net return to farmers in the United States. But to have blocked such a sale on short notice in the absence of acute shortages at home would have been a departure from two centuries of a policy of vigorously selling our farm products abroad. In 1974, more than 20 billion dollars worth of farm produce were exported. Without this trade, the United States balance of payments would be in a catastrophic state. Indeed the economy which at times is already on the ropes would be knocked completely out of the ring. I can think of no greater disincentive to farmers for maximizing productivity than the threat of an export ban every time prices showed prospects of increasing. A planned strategic grain reserve for possible lean years is a different matter. At the time it goes into storage, it should be earmarked "for domestic emergencies only" and considered apart from the grain in domestic and international commerce.

What a difference an inch or two of June rain in the Russian wheat country might have made! Or how different things might have been had Russia had a reasonable reserve to tide her over. There is a lesson here for every country. Lean years are inevitable, and without food reserves, increasing prices and sometimes hunger are also inevitable. Because Russia has some money, the effects spilled over to the United States and from there to the world grain market in general. There is currently much discussion of the need for an international grain reserve. Possibly something can be worked out under United Nations auspices. Meanwhile, I think each government has responsibility for a minimum reserve earmarked for its own people and set up in such a way that it would have minimum effect on the normal grain economy.

In the United States, for example, I believe we should have, 400 million bushels of bread grain (about two bushels for each person) in a rotating reserve. As old grain was sold to avoid quality deterioration, new crop grain would take its place. If the world knew that this reserve was only for domestic emergencies there should be a minimum impact on grain prices. Such a program might cost two dollars per person per year for interest and storage. In my book, the United States, like the rest of the world, has been running perilously close to the danger level with respect to grain reserves and I think two dollars per capita to contribute to an adequate food supply in the event of a long drought would be a good investment.

Of course, countries with both grain production and a poultry or livestock industry can reduce their animal numbers and thus divert both meat and the grain that would otherwise be fed to human consumption. This is an important safety factor and one that Russia has taken advantage of in earlier years of a short grain crop. She chose not to do so in 1972 since the money and credit were available to purchase enough from abroad to keep her livestock enterprises intact. Although lowering of our consumption of meat as some are suggesting, might be desirable, I think a drastic reduction in our animal industries should be only a backup safety valve. The first line of defense against a drought year like 1936 should be a food grain reserve in each country.

Food costs seem to lead the inflation parade and it is difficult to see how they can be stabilized so long as the supply of bread grain and feed grain is no more than equal to demand. Under existing conditions a short crop in any major producing country can have a world-wide price effect. Even the threat of poor crops in the absence of a reserve seems to help keep the inflationary fires burning. Nothing could contribute more to reducing the threat of further inflation than stocks of grain for food and feed somewhat in excess of demand. Farmers are doing their best to produce more but they may not be able to move faster than increases in demand.

The remaining approach to building a reserve is the obvious one of a reduction in animal protein intake. This is being talked about primarily as a way of making grain available for relief purposes but there is also an economic aspect. If enough people in the affluent world cut their grain-fed meat consumption by even 10 to 15 percent, the resulting lower demand for grain for livestock would go a long way toward keeping food prices from increasing further. Actually this seems to be happening at this writing in 1975, no doubt as a response to a lower level of economic activity.

The economic effect of eating less meat would not be permanent. Even with a lower consumption per capita, population growth would soon bring us back to the present total meat demand. But it should materially help stem the current tide of inflation and give agricultural productivity a chance to catch up. Of course, a sudden further reduction in meat demand could have a devastating effect on livestock industries but the human appetite being what it is, such a shift in diet is unlikely to happen overnight. Nutritionists would say that aside from contributing to inflation controls, many would be more healthy if they reduced their meat consumption. Unfortunately, many even in the more affluent world get insufficient protein and others have only a marginally adequate diet. I am hopeful that any long-term reduction in per capita meat consumption would not apply to them.

Water erosion such as shown above can literally carry our future food production capacity down the river. Much erodable land has been converted to permanent pasture (below) in recent years with a resulting great reduction in erosion. Contour planting, terracing and no-tillage farming are other approaches to keep sloping soil in place.

5

Ecology Down on The Farm

Whether we like it or not, farmers are the custodians of a very sizable portion of the world's land surface. Much of the earth's ecological well-being depends on how they manage the soil and the vegetation that covers it. Actually, farmers were the first environmentalists. I remember my grandfather seeding down a slope for permanent pasture because there was too much soil runoff when planted to corn. He wanted to reduce silting of a nearby stream as well as preserve his land.

But my grandfather was not among the first to have concern for soil runoff. A highlight of a week my wife and I spent on the Spanish Mediterranean Coast was an opportunity to see and hike along stone terraces build by Roman settlers over two thousand years ago. Some of them may have been erected by the Phoenicians long before that. The land held in place by terraces is still planted to grapes, olives and vegetables. A Spanish agronomist estimated that with the present use of fertilizer this land is now more productive than it has ever been in the past, and where well managed the soil is actually being improved in physical properties. Even older terraces than these are still being used in several parts of the world.

Of course, few ancient farmers had the knowledge or capability of conserving soil and reducing runoff. Otherwise there would not have been such devastating erosion particularly in the Mediterranean Region. But the seeds of conservation farming were there and they began to sprout and send down roots which led to our present concepts and practices as discussed in chapter 3. Farmers generally are now more soil-conservation conscious than ever before. Of course, they have much to learn, and where population pressures are too great, carrying out sound land management practices is difficult. Without fertilization and resulting vigorous plant growth, it is hard to maintain good soil structure let alone the building of fertility. In the industrial countries we have the knowledge and the materials available so there is no excuse for not improving our soils.

To be sure, there are some current farm practices that need modification in the interests of the environment. But if you remember the horrendous soil erosion of thirty years or more ago with the resulting excessive silting of streams, I think you will agree that agriculture has made tremendous strides in environmental improvement. Let's look at ecology down on the farm, both the old place as many of us remember it and also farms of the 1970's.

Environmental Benefits of Modern Farm Practices

Not long ago I hiked over some charming hillsides in the Bald Mountain Recreation Area near Detroit. A wide range of trees, shrubs and wild flowers, to say nothing of innumerable songbirds, exemplified the semi-wild but accessible land that we increasingly need close to our cities. I had seen this same rolling country about fifty years ago when my father farmed some of the same fields. Later, on a visit to Lee County, Alabama, where I lived in the 1930's as a young man on the agricultural staff at Auburn University, I was astonished to see how many former worn-out corn and cotton fields had grown up to vigorous pines, some nearly saw log in size. Thinning for pulpwood was in progress. Interspersed among the blocks of trees were lush pastures supporting sleek cattle, a marked contrast to the undernourished critters I remember. By using modern methods of reforestation and establishing improved pasture grasses with fertilization to restore the soil's mineral deficiencies, eroded hillsides had been covered with protective vegetation.

These hills in Michigan and Alabama were no longer losing silt to adjacent streams with each rain, and their earlier feeble contribution to our food and fiber supply had been replaced with a meaningful addition to beef production and forest resources as well as to wildlife and outdoor recreation. How was all this possible when we have tens of millions more people to feed and export more agricultural products than when the hills were being farmed? The answer? Vastly better yields! We can now produce our needs plus an abundance for export on less land than was used 30 years ago. Using U.S. Department of Agriculture statistics, I calculated the greater acreage that would be required to produce our major crops at their recent annual volume if we still obtained the yields of the period 1938-40. The figure added up to more than 300 million acres, an area equal to all of the southeastern United States. A crop acreage increase of even half this magnitude would involve land highly subject to erosion, the very hills we are now converting to forests, recreational areas and the soil-protecting sod of permanent pastures.

Today's high yields are equated with close plant spacing and vigorous growth. More unharvested portions of plants including roots are left in and on the soil when crops are highly productive. These heavier crop residues contribute to an improved physical condition of the soil, better rainfall penetration, and reduced erosion. Thus, recent yield increases have helped to conserve the land that is still farmed as well as that which has been diverted to noncrop uses.

Of course, not all ecological influences of modern crop production have been advantageous. If the several recently identified pollution problems can be solved, farmers and agricultural technologists will have made a significant additional contribution to environmental quality. Much has already been accomplished through research and regulation in limiting the use of persistent and bioconcentrated pesticides and in replacing them with ecologically safer materials. Now we need to see that overregulation does not discourage industry from continuing its search for safer and more effective agricultural chemicals. If there is public and private collaboration on adequate but sensible safety evaluations, crop producers of the future can have better pest management programs based on chemicals integrated with other methods of control. Pesticides in relation to the environment will be discussed further in chapter 6.

The extent to which fertilizer contributes to accelerated eutrophication as a result of runoff or leaching is still under investigation. Intensive cropping with close stands and quick succession of one crop following another as now being practiced wherever moisture conditions permit tend to minimize fertilizer losses to ground water or streams, as do modern erosion control practices such as strip cropping, terracing, and reduced tillage. Where fertilizer losses are indeed found to be a significant contributor to eutrophication or where ground water pollution may occur, some farm practices will have to be changed.

Nitrogen compounds are of primary concern with respect to leaching and there is a lot of new technology under development which, if ultimately put to use, will greatly reduce the chances of movement to ground or surface water. Some of these developments are coated fertilizer, nitrification control, and nitrate removal from impounded irrigation tailings. Without these, side dressing with fertilizer after the crop has emerged in lieu of preplant application may have to be more widely practiced. This minimizes the chances of nitrate leaching before plant roots are there to take it up. Some further aspects of fertilizer and the environment will be discussed in the following chapter.

Burning of crop residues resulting in a contribution to air pollution is already a thing of the past in many areas. For this we can thank a better understanding of the importance of organic matter to soil fertility, to the availability of nitrogen fertilizer necessary to support the decomposition of crop residues, and, in some instances, to new short-strawed grain varieties. Research on the utilization of heavy straws such as from rice, which do not decay readily when incorporated with the soil may further point the way toward a cleaner atmosphere. The availability of non-protein nitrogen feed supplements is making it practical to feed more straw and other agricultural wastes to livestock. Current research on ways to make the fiber in farm wastes more digestible to cattle is likely to pay off.

I believe that of all the environmental problems down on the farm, soil erosion is still the most serious. Man's first major insult to the environment, which goes back to the very beginning of agriculture, was the loss of soil and the pollution of water with silt carried in runoff from overgrazed pastures or sloping crop land. Every pound of soil lost from agricultural land means that much less for future food production. Although farmers do have a long way to go in erosion control, tremendous progress has been made during the past few decades through terracing, strip cropping, and the establishment of sod drainage channels. Stubble mulch farming, now widely practiced in semi-arid areas, has greatly reduced the likelihood of wind erosion. New minimum tillage and zero tillage farming methods are making further contributions to the protection of soil from erosion.

If you drive through hilly country, particularly in the southeastern portion of the United States you will see innumerable farm ponds mostly build during the last 40 years. Most of them contain fish and thus provide both food and recreation. Many are used for stock watering and irrigation. All hold back water from rapid runoff during heavy rains and are thus a factor in reducing flooding downstream. There are over two million such ponds in the United States built by farmers with the assistance of public funds. In total they have a very meaningful environmental as well as an economic and social effect. Ponds provide water for wildlife as well as stock and they obviously contribute to a diversity of the environment and encourage a wide range of life forms.   Before you criticize farmers too severely for the environmental mistakes you believe they have made, ask yourself, "When did I get out in the heat and the mud on my tractor and excavate a hole in the ground and build a levee to create a pond?   When did I last plant the fringes of a pond with desirable woody plants and fertilize the water to promote the aquatic plant life that starts the food chain that ultimately results in edible fish?"

In recent years my work has frequently taken me to the vast Great Plains of the United States and Canada and I am continually impressed with the growth of windbreaks around farm buildings.   My first trip through this country, which originally supported only grass, was in 1932 when the idea of windbreaks and shelterbelts was just taking hold.   Now I see a world of difference, with well-developed windbreaks around many farmsteads.

The monotony of endless grasslands is illustrated by a recollection of my wife's parents who homesteaded near Glendive, Montana, before the turn of the century.   If you wanted a meeting place in town "the tree" was a well-known spot.   A number of hardy species seem to do well in the dry plains, given a little care to get them started.   In higher rainfall areas woody plants take over if land is left idle, but in the Plains you have to coax a young tree and farmers have done a lot of coaxing of windbreak plantings since the area was first settled.

Shortly before writing these words, I was in the Red River Valley of Manitoba.   It was a good year and the country, although flat, was truly beautiful.   In addition to waving fields of wheat and barley, the flax, sunflower, rapeseed and buckwheat were all in bloom.   Their blue, gold, canary yellow and white flowers made a spectacular contrast to the green of the late-planted grain and the gold of the early seedings which were approaching harvest time.   But the windbreaks stood out, the stately rows of Blue Spruce, Ash, Boxelder and Russian Olive.   I spent an hour wandering through one windbreak next to the wheat land I was using for some experimental plots and was astonished at the number of birds I counted. There were several species one would rarely see in the open prairie, ones that like woody plant habitat interspersed with open fields. Surely the farmers that nursed these windbreak trees many years ago made a valuable contribution to a more diverse environment in the 1970's.

Wildlife On The Farm

Several years ago when selective herbicides for woody plant control were relatively new, I was asked by a county extension agent in a dairy region of northeastern United States to talk to a group of farmers. The assigned topic, "New Ways to Control Brush," was very timely for this group. Few farmers of the area had ever done a good job of managing their pastures for maximum yield of nutritious forage, the starting point for the milk, cream and butter on your table. Hawthorn and bramble thickets choked out the grass on large areas of the otherwise fertile hillside pastures. Willows and alder dominated the bottom lands and assorted scrub, unpalatable to cattle, was scattered throughout most grazing areas.

An agronomist from the state university preceded me on the program on the subject of pasture fertilization for increased forage production. My opening gun was, "Are you going to fertilize grass and clover or are you just going to promote more and bigger brush?" I told them how they could use the basal bark treatment with a brush killer in diesel oil for individual plants and how to spray the foliage of thickets safely and effectively with a material that would not adversely affect the limited grass that was there but allow it, along with supplemental seeding, to take over. I am sure many of them left the meeting with plans to try out the then new basal bark method of brush control, so well adapted to use during the winter or early spring when farmers can find the time for jobs not directly related to crop production. I went away with the satisfaction of having passed along some useful new technology which, if put to work by these dairy farmers, could make it possible for them to produce more milk without increasing the size of their farms and thus contribute to a continuing abundant supply of dairy products for the consumer.

The next day there was a story in the local paper, the gist of which was well summarized by the headline, "Agronomist Recommends Farmers Kill Brush." The following day all hell broke loose and I learned the hard way about the conflict of interests between the farmer and the hunter, better known as the sportsman. The "outdoor" columnist of the paper took me to task for promoting the destruction of game cover and there were letters to the editor on the same theme. The divergence of farmer interests and those of nonhunting people was emphasized by a letter from an Audubon Society member who decried the elimination of diverse vegetation types thus discouraging a greater variation in bird species inhabiting an area.

Hawthorn was mentioned in the news article as one of the species I had incriminated as a robber of water, nutrients and sunlight that should go to the production of grass and clover. A wildflower lover wrote me that I should be ashamed of myself for suggesting that anyone kill a beautiful hawthorn tree. I could only reply that I so appreciated this plant that I had two of them growing in my yard, but that farmers had acquired their land and pay their rent or taxes on it each year for the express purpose of raising forage for their cattle and that grass and clover will hardly grow at all in the dense shade of a spreading hawthorn. I soon realized there were no arguments to be won so I ducked and maintained as low a profile as possible. The incident did give me insight into some conceptions and misconceptions prevailing on both sides of the farm ecology argument. Here are views held by different groups.

The hunter naturally wants more game to shoot. He perceives numerous overgrown fence rows, incompletely harvested crops and pastures with scattered brush as the best habitat for a high population of pheasants, rabbits and other game species that one may find in farming areas.

The nature lover is interested in having a wide range of bird species, wild flowers and diverse woody vegetation throughout the countryside. Like the hunter, he deplores clean fence rows and pastures devoted exclusively to the production of grass and clover. He would have each farm set aside a woodlot or other unused area for the promotion of diverse forms of life. Many birds and other wildlife thrive best at the edge of wooded areas and nature lovers see many small parcels, ideally one on each farm, as more effective in promoting wildlife than a few large wooded areas.

The far-our environmentalist combines the thinking of the nature lover with an antipathy toward intensive crop and livestock production. He tends to be against the use of fertilizers and crop protection chemicals and the term monoculture is high on his list of dirty words. By monoculture, he means large areas devoted to a single crop. Some would have us return to the mixed cropping system practiced years ago when pumpkins and beans often grew in the cornfield.

The farmer, like all of us, has to make a living, but he knows people have to eat and there is no way they can keep from going hungry if he doesn't produce food in abundance. He is really striving to keep his soil from running down the river and to improve its fertility. After all, his soil is his bank account for the future. The farmer likes to hunt, too, but except for a few game culture specialists, pheasants don't help pay the bills. City hunters are more often than not a nuisance. Remember those gates left open and fences broken down?

A woodlot or unproductive corner of the farm left to nature is favored by many farmers, but at the present price of posts and fencing not to mention the value of land a brushy pasture can be a loser for a cattle grower. Aside from economic considerations in areas of high rainfall, a sod pasture gives the best protection against erosion. It has been shown that soil loss is considerably greater when heavy rain falls on a shrub-infested pasture than where there is a thick sod. Because so few sod-forming herbaceous plants will grow in the shade of shrubs and trees the soil tends to be partially bare and this makes it a "sitting duck" for erosive rain.

Ranchers in drier rangeland country recognize that certain palatable shrubs do have a place in good management. The key to profitable livestock raising combined with good conservation is management to fit a particular soil and climatic situation. In the view of most farmers, however, fence rows choked with woody brush just don't make sense. It's not just the land occupied but the roots that grow out into adjacent fields. A six-foot sumac bush can put out 30-foot roots and rob a crop of water and nutrients.

Windbreaks and farm ponds are favored by most farmers because of their utility combined with their support of diverse life forms. Farm people don't dispute the naturalists' claim that birds aid in the control of some kinds of insects but he doubts they are of much help with most of his serious pests. If there is a potentially costly crop insect problem, such as corn root worm, green bug of wheat or potato leaf hopper, all the birds in the world won't put food on the supermarket shelf. And when considering habitat favorable for the beneficial birds he can't forget the destructive ones, the hordes that flock into fruit plantings and grain fields just before harvest time.

The farmer doesn't look upon himself as the custodian of wildlife for sportsmen and urban recreationists but he knows that a number of economically sound operations, such as the establishment of living windbreaks, the construction of ponds, rotational grazing, and the encouragement of winter stubble and cover crops also provide favorable wildlife habitat as a bonus value. Gleaning the fields of waste grain after harvest affords many a song and game bird a sustaining ration.

An Environmental Goal for Modern Farms

Obviously not all the farm management ideas put forth by the hunters, nature lovers and environmentalists can be adopted by today's farmers but these groups have some legitimate concerns and ideas worthy of careful study. Ecologically speaking, much about modern farming is good but much needs improvement. There may be no way to completely meld farmers' concepts on how land should be managed with those of nonfarm people. But with a little give and take we should be able to come up with goals that point in the direction of sound economics together with land management for the greatest public good, and at the same time help assure your future food supply. Here is my attempt at a statement of such goals.

1. Make farming enterprises as productive as possible consistent with the environmental protection goals which follow. Only by achieving high agricultural productivity can land be available for recreation and nature and hunting preserves. Without high productivity, we will need all our land just for raising food.
2. Keep soil in place. Every particle that runs off or blows away contributes to water and air pollution and is no longer there for future food production. We all have a responsibility to see that our better lands are reserved for agriculture but the farmer has an equal responsibility to manage it for perpetual productivity and to reduce pollution to a minimum.
3. Protect crops and livestock with approved methods. When drugs and pesticides are involved labels should be followed scrupulously. Prior to approval and registration, officials determine safety to people and to the environment but safety tests are based on the printed label directions and not some other method of use.
4. Utilize organic wastes on the farm to the fullest extent practicable to improve soil structure and fertility. Otherwise dispose of them in a way that pollution will be minimized if not eliminated. The best place for manure is back on the land but if recycling it is uneconomic it should be disposed of through lagooning or some other approved method.

5. Follow crop rotation and husbandry practices that will keep the land covered with vegetation as much of the time as possible and at the same time aid in soil fertility improvement and promote maximum productivity.
6. Leave some part of the farm in a wild or semi-wild state to help promote wildlife diversity. This may be a woodlot, an unproductive piece of ground ill-adapted to crop or pasture, a pond or in the prairies a planted windbreak.

Now that we have some goals, how do farmers measure up? I have visited a lot of farms in many parts of North America and Europe during the last few years and often I can spot some practices that fall short of these goals but more often most farm practices appear ecologically sound. There is risk in fall plowing in the corn belt of land that is subject to blowing, but then there is also stubble mulching on millions of acres where wind erosion was serious before this conservation practice became widespread. There is far too much wind erosion on the loessial soils of Idaho and Eastern Washington and Oregon. There is still some tillage on hillsides that are bound to erode in heavy rains but then there are the millions of acres of former hilly crop land now planted to permanent pasture or trees. One still sees too much overgrazing but the majority of our livestock people are in the business for keeps and are learning how to manage their pastures without erosion. One farmer carelessly emptied surplus insecticide spray into a stream and killed some fish, but tens of thousands have used the same insecticide sensibly and safely following label precautions and directions. Unfortunately population pressures in many less developed areas are fostering ecologically unsound land-management practices. Severe overgrazing in the sub-Sahara region and deforestation followed by unsound tillage practices on the southern slopes of the Himalayas are examples. The severe erosion in parts of Latin America could be corrected with the soil conservation approaches taken for granted in North America.

In Conclusion, those who raise crops and livestock for their livelihood together with the scientists and technologists who serve them are the inevitable custodians of a considerable part of the earth's land surface. As a result of recent increases in yields they have contributed much to a better environment through the release of land to optional uses. Reduced acreage, soil conservation practices, and more intensive cropping have all contributed to less erosion and the concomitant silting of streams. We have come a long way through research and regulation toward modifying pest control programs to achieve environmental safety. Research projects underway on other forms of environmental pollution related to agriculture show great promise of making further positive contributions to a better environment and I am confident that farmers will put them to work.

New pollution problems have arisen as a result of a great increase in concentrated livestock and poultry production. These are far better understood than they were even five years ago, and environmentally sound waste disposal programs, often backed by regulations, are becoming more common. At a modest increase in cost to the consumer of meat, eggs and dairy products these waste handling methods can become universal. Waste disposal by food processing plants, now rigidly regulated in many countries, has been largely converted to methods that will have minimum adverse effects on the environment.

The old conflict between the food producer on one hand and wildlife and nature interests on the other may never be completely resolved. No doubt many farmers can do more to encourage wildlife, but let us not overlook their significant contributions in recent years through increasing yields which have allowed the luxury of much land to be set aside just for wildlife preservation. Let's not overlook the woodlots they have left standing and the millions of ponds and windbreaks they have constructed.

With the recent increase in crop acreage made necessary by greater food demand and the depletion of reserves, there is great risk that land ill-suited to tillage will be converted from pastures or other uses. Erosion is inevitably more severe on sloping land and if it is put in cultivation a new effort at contour farming and the establishment of terraces will be necessary.

I am sure the work of the Soil Conservation Service in the United States and similar organizations elsewhere is not finished. Much land once farmed but now in forest or pasture never should be tilled.

The high consumption of feed grains in the more prosperous world has come in for much criticism recently because of food shortages in many less-developed countries. Occasionally some ill-informed observer predicts that we will have to stop raising sheep and cattle because they are such inefficient converters of feed. These prophets overlook the fact that ruminant animals can convert grass and other forage to nutritious human food and that this rough feed is a renewable resource that can be grown on land not well-suited to any other kind of food production.

Actually, no more than twenty million of the world's billion or more cattle are "on feed" at any one time. Most beef animals outside North America are grass fed and even there a significant proportion of slaughter animals move from pasture directly to the packing plant, particularly when grain is scarce and its price is high. Even though some grain may be utilized during the final months of finishing to obtain more tender meat, it is misleading to condemn bovine animals on the implication that they are fed grain throughout their life. Actually, many have reached 70 to 80 percent of their growth when grain feeding begins, so the amount fed per unit of dressed weight is modest. It is often overlooked by critics of beef animal finishing that there is always much grain of poor quality because of adverse weather at harvest time, and this is really only suited to live-stock consumption. Such grain may have nearly its full nutritive value but is unsuited to processing for human food. It should also be remembered that cattle consume many agricultural and food processing wastes and by-products.

There is a trend toward finishing beef largely on high-yielding silage made from the entire above ground corn plant harvested after the grain has stored its full quota of food substances but before the crop is dry. Average yields of corn silage exceeded 13 tons per acre in the United States over the past five years.

Those with concern for the amount of grain fed to cattle that might otherwise be available for food aid programs can take comfort in these recent trends especially when one recognizes that on conversion to beef an acre of silage will result in total edible protein that compares favorably in quantity and is of better quality than the protein produced by the average acre of wheat or dry edible beans.

With the right kind of pasture management, land that would be subject to erosion if tilled can produce nutritious and delicious beef indefinitely without soil loss. Then if some crop land is devoted to grain or silage for finishing to improve meat quality, it is a reasonable price to pay for the vast benefit of the ruminant animal's ability to convert forage from rough land to human food. Ecologically speaking, I think the continuing production of cattle and sheep on well-managed pastures is imperative.

Corn grown by the author in an early no-tillage test (1951). An old sod was killed with herbicides before planting and subsequent weeds selectively controlled with a post-emergence chemical treatment. Today several million acres of hilly land are being protected from erosion and made more productive by no-tillage methods.

6

The Hunger Mongers

There are a number of influences abroad
in the land that are tending to hold back
agricultural productivity. During the recent years of farm surpluses these did not
concern us and in some instances they were
thought to be good. Why worry about
efficient food production when our storages were filled to overflowing? From now
on those who discourage food productivity, even with the best of intentions for
our welfare, will be candidates for the title,
Hunger Monger. Of course, there may again
be periods of surpluses of one commodity
or another but probably of only short dura-
tion. Farmers should not be hamstrung
in their capability to produce an abundance using as few precious resources as
possible. Our future depends so much on
that capability that it should be nurtured
in every way possible. Aside from insuring adequate nutrition for all there is little
hope of curing inflation if food is scarce.
Who are the Hunger Mongers, those who invite disaster unknowingly by discouraging
or actually blocking efficient food production in one way or another?

The Land Gobblers

On a recent visit to my home town where a large majority live in single family dwellings, a friend from the Netherlands commented on the luxury of our spacious yards. In his country, as you may have seen, a high proportion of people live in apartments and only postage stamp grounds surround what single houses there are. As their cities push out, farms scheduled to be displaced continue to produce food until apartment construction actually begins. He exclaimed, "If we had as broad highways and as many parks and golf courses and as much land around our houses as you do in America, I am sure we would all go hungry."

The New World has always been able to use land extravagantly. First there was more land than people could possibly use and then the yield revolution released much land once in farms for optional uses. But now is the time to look ahead. Land-use planning is very much in vogue these days and nothing we can do to assure the kind of future we want is more important. Most states and many smaller units of government have land-use planning commissions but unfortunately, for the most part, they have been giving little attention to food production needs for the future. They have agriculture on their list of factors to be studied and they may even give lip service to reserving the best land for farms, but there has been little zoning for permanent agriculture. Cities continue their sprawl, often in the direction of our most productive land. Developers like the economy of level terrain. Shopping centers and single story industrial buildings, all with their tremendous parking lot requirements, are more cheaply built on level land, which is often best adapted to food production.

Aside from ever-mushrooming urban development, nonagricultural and nonforest demands on our land have been growing at a faster clip than population. Millions of acres are devoted to corridor right-of-ways (highways, pipelines, transmission lines and railroads). The United States now has 200 million acres set aside for recreational and conservation purposes. This includes National Parks, National Wildlife Refuges, Wild and Scenic Rivers, National Seashores, State Game Lands, etc. While much of this acreage is unsuited for agriculture, appreciable portions are. For example, the most recent acquisition of the National Wildlife Refuge System is a 220,000 acre ranch some sixty miles south of Albuquerque.

It appears that the Congress of the United States is being pressured by environmental groups and hunting enthusiasts to outlaw livestock grazing on public lands. Such action could reduce production of sheep by nine million and cattle by five million head on tens of millions of acres. Aside from grazing fees which go to the public treasury, we have long benefited from the greater supply of meat and wool made possible by raising livestock on lands administered by the Forest Service and the Bureau of Land Management. There have, no doubt, been abuses in the past and these should be corrected. That part of the public domain suitable for grazing can be wisely managed for multiple uses to encourage wildlife and provide for recreation at the same time the more productive grasslands are utilized by stock. These lands and the vegetation they produce belong to all citizens, the wearers of clothing and eaters of food. Those pushing Congress to reserve them for narrow interests are, in my view, the greatest potential land gobblers of all time.

In a sense most of us have been land gobblers. With huge surpluses there was no reason to be concerned, but that is water over the dam. Now is the time to take stock of future needs for crop and pasture land. Should we not permanently zone our best for agriculture? What is wrong with having city and country interspersed with farms near or even surrounded by urban development. There is much talk among urban planners about the virtue of greenbelts but these need not be in forests if the soil is productive and of suitable terrain for crops or pastures. Air purification benefits can still be realized if the greenbelt is a band of farmland. True, some crops suffer from automobile exhaust fumes but others are less particular. Crop plants can even help purify the city air by assimilating carbon monoxide in addition to the carbon dioxide they use along with water as a building block for photosynthesis.

Population will continue to increase for some time even though in the United States we may have reached an average family size that would eventually result in zero growth. Cities will continue to expand and there will be many demands on the land for recreational facilities, industry and transportation. Land-use planning is going to be very important to our future and I think there are several objectives the planners should have in the interests of the kind and quality of food we hope our grandchildren can enjoy:

1. Direct urban growth toward the poorer agricultural land insofar as possible.
2. Where expansion must occupy good land intersperse urban development with broad strips zoned permanently for agriculture. Aside from pure air benefits, raising high value crops near centers of population will minimize energy requirements for refrigeration and transportation, and labor for harvesting should be more readily available.
3. Plan airports, highways and pipeline and electric right-of ways so the grassed areas can be harvested for hay or silage. I recently saw hay being baled along major highways in North Dakota. With the right grading, preferably at the time of construction, this could be done in many places.
4. Make a permanent zoning commitment for livestock enterprises. Too often producers have been forced to move because of odor complaints only to have the ever-expanding city encroach on their new location with the same old complaints. A buffer zone designated only for cropping may be a solution.
5. In planning large recreational areas on land suitable for pasture consider interspersal of public and private land. Remember the "edge effect" and its benefit to wildlife. There is no reason why a large preserve must be in a solid block.

If the best soil is devoted to fenced pasture the remainder will be just as useful and may actually support more wildlife and be more attractive than if in solid woods or unused grassland.

The Soil Despoilers

If you were around during the New Deal days of the 1930's you may remember when the United States Soil Conservation Service was formed. We had been experiencing "Dust Bowl" conditions in the West, and the Southeast was literally running down the river. Both wind and water erosion are natural processes but man's disturbance of the soil's vegetative cover, often using farming methods ill-adapted to rolling terrain, or to prolonged periods of dry, windy weather, had resulted in an acceleration that threatened the very future of these lands. Farmers didn't use these unsound practices through carelessness. They just didn't understand conservation farming.

Through education and leadership in the establishment of sound agricultural practices, the Soil Conservation Service has led the way over the past few decades to the far healthier situation we have today. You have seen the results in hilly country of terraced fields, grassed waterways and contour cropping. Not so obvious is the stubble mulching and other modified tillage practices in drier areas that have made the recurrence of the Dust Bowl of the 1930's most unlikely. All this has been helped tremendously by the yield revolution which permitted converting the more erodable land to permanent pasture and forests.

Not all the excess silt in our streams or dust in the air results from inept farming methods. Often it is due to careless management of soil being graded for highways or development projects. But there are still despoilers mismanaging some of our precious farmland. You still see fields that should be terraced or contour farmed with rows running up and down the slope. There are still farmers using the moleboard plow in areas where stubble mulching would give good protection against wind erosion in the event of a long drought. Fall plowing is often a necessity if crops are to be produced in large acreages, but on some light soils it is ecologically unwise. In the winter and spring you can see soil drifting over the surface and into drainage ditches where the accumulated silt is ready to go down to the closest stream with the first heavy rain.

There is a wealth of knowledge, much of it gained in very recent years, on how to manage soil with very minimum exposure to erosion, for example, the new minimum tillage and zero-tillage concepts. Growers who are determining the adaptability of these new methods to their soil and farming system are among the fertility builders doing their part to assure future food supply. Thankfully, fertility builders are now in the vast majority. I believe the remaining soil despoilers will soon disappear as more and more farmers are recognizing that soil conservation methods are the ones that give the greatest long range economic return. Even more important, they are recognizing that conserving soil is not enough. Fertility building with optimum fertilization and keeping crops growing vigorously throughout as much of the year as possible also pay off.

The Organic Farming Promoters

I am a great believer in soil organic matter. All of my grass clippings find a use as a mulch for my asparagus and raspberry beds and even the autumn leaves go into a compost pile to later be worked into the garden. This keeps my soil in good physical condition but I also apply a fertilizer to get the mineral nutrients my plants need for optimum growth. As important as organic matter is to good soil tilth it is virtually impossible to supply all the essential mineral nutrients from organic sources. Of course, if you have an abundance of manure available you can get most required nutrients from it, but on many soils you will still need to apply superphosphate to achieve a good mineral balance.

If you like to garden strictly organically you can have fun and probably raise some good crops. Finding organic supplements in sizable amounts per unit area of soil being tilled is relatively easy for a modest garden but quite another matter for a farm. Not that organic matter is less important to farming operations, but except where manure is available in quantity there is no practical way to get it except to grow it in place. Crop residues, both roots and tops, add large amounts of organic material to the soil and the more vigorous the crop and the more frequently the land is used the more plant material remains to insure good tilth. Big crops take large amounts of minerals for their nourishment and the more quickly one crop follows another the more minerals required. There is no practical way to accomplish good crop nutrition except to apply appropriate amounts of fertilizer.

Commercial organic farming is a different matter than just gardening. I think the promoters of organic farming and food fadists who support their concepts are doing a great disservice to future generations. They are some of the Hunger Mongers, not recognizing the impact they have but having it nonetheless. There is simply no way people today or in the future can be fed without the use of fertilizer and without crop and livestock protection chemicals as a part of integrated disease and pest control programs. The religious fervor some organic people exhibit is bound to rub off on folks who have little understanding of how plants grow and how the public is protected from harmful chemical residues through regulatory laws. If much of the world adopted the system of farming they recommend, we would soon have a serious food shortage. This is not to say that manure should not be applied to the soil whenever available. That is the most ecologically sound way to handle it. But if all the manure generated by our livestock was divided up among the acres tilled we would still have a crisis in plant nutrition if fertilizer was not used. Indeed, we would have a food disaster, a horrendous famine. To be sure, fertilizer has sometimes been used unwisely, but these instances are growing fewer all the time as farmers learn more about how to employ it with the greatest benefit to crop plants and with minimum loss to the environment. At the present high cost of fertilizer, growers have every incentive to use it wisely.

If you are sold on organic gardening and farming I can imagine some loud sputtering at this point. I am sure there are no arguments to be won, but rather than to say more, I would like to quote some comments made recently by Dr. John Carew, Chairman of the Department of Horticulture at Michigan State University.

Most plants "feed" themselves on inorganic minerals (nitrogen, phosphorus, potassium, etc.) taken in thorough the roots. Nothing passes through the cell walls of the roots in an organic form. "Plants don't eat; they drink." All organic matter must be first decomposed to a chemical state before it moves into the plant. Research has repeatedly shown that plant nutrients derived from compost or other organic material are no better nor worse than those from chemical fertilizers.

Plants grown organically are supposed to be more resistant to diseases and insects. According to this theory, "well fed" plants are less likely to be attacked and are better able to ward off diseases. This claim generally arises from the observation that home gardens have fewer disease and insect problems than commercial farms. This is true, but more because of the intensive nature of commercial farming and the market demands for blemish-free fruits and vegetables. It is not really due to the presence or absence of chemical fertilizers.

In many respects plants are like people; a well-balanced diet will prevent most *nutritional* disorders but will have little influence on susceptibility to certain pathogenic diseases such as chicken pox or influenza in man or fusarium wilt, aster yellows or seed maggot infestations in plants. Whether the plant gets its nutrients from organic or chemical sources seems to have no effect on disease or insect attack.

Natural or biological means of avoiding, repelling or controlling insects, diseases and weeds are preferred. Crop rotation, natural predators, scheduling planting dates to avoid pests, mixed cropping, disease resistant varieties, mulching and the like, often contribute to reduced pest problems.

Frequently, however, they are only *partially* effective; i.e., infestations may be reduced 50, 60 or 80 percent but seldom 95 or 100 percent. In seasons when natural insect infestations are high biological control methods might mean 3 wormy ears instead of 10 in a dozen sweet corn or 2 worms per head of broccoli instead of 10.

Some garden crops, for example, tomatoes, carrots, squash, cherries, strawberries and raspberries, can be grown in many years without protection from pesticides. Many others, including cabbage, radishes, onions and apples are subject to numerous insects and diseases which are not adequately controlled by natural means.

Some people claim that organically grown foods taste better. There is little basis for proving or disproving the statement. Organic gardeners often compare their fruits and vegetables with those available in local supermarkets. Actually, they are comparing food carefully picked at its peak of quality with products that may have been harvested 7 or more days earlier. This shipped-in food probably lost some of its quality in transit or on display. Comparisons between *home-grown* fruits and vegetables, raised either organically or with properly used chemical fertilizers and pesticides, seldom reveal taste differences.

The claim is sometimes made that organically grown foods are more healthful. Evaluating this claim is difficult. Comparing the mineral and vitamin contents of both types reveal no consistent differences. As a matter of fact, crops grown hydroponically (in sand or gravel and fertilized only with soluble chemical fertilizers in the total absence of organic matter) have nutrient compositions similar to plants grown organically at the same time and location.

There can be no disputing those who say they *feel better* as a result of gardening organically or buying organic foods. Medical authorities are well aware that a person's physical well-being can be strongly influenced by his mental attitude and his personal faith in the value of certain foods.

Gardening is fun, organically or otherwise. I will not try to sell you on fertilizer or pesticides, but I hope you will not try to sell large scale organic methods when their adoption would most certainly contribute to future hunger.

The Safety-at-any-Cost People

Equipment to reduce exhaust emissions on automobiles costs money. Now we find that our more expensive cars require more gasoline and mileage may be reduced by as much as 25 percent. So our diminishing petroleum supplies are disappearing at a faster rate. Ralph Nader finds safety hazards in small automobiles and thus encourages heavier vehicles with their higher gasoline consumption. So we have trade-offs. Chances are that the U.S. Congress, the Environmental Protection Agency and even Nader himself did not visualize the net effects of greater safety and atmospheric pollution control. Perhaps they would have made the same decisions anyway, but would it not have been better if all the factors had been weighed at the beginning?

Now the safety-at-any-cost people are tampering with our food supply. Let's understand the nature of the trade-offs in advance. We can live with more expensive cars and if supplies of petroleum become critical we can probably make it last through tight rationing while we learn to harness other sources of energy. But let's not wake up some morning and find that safety measures of questionable necessity have in fact reduced our food supply and thus contributed to the most unsafe situation man can face, a marginally adequate food supply or worse yet, an actual shortage.

There are groups stalking legislative halls and the offices of regulatory agencies which would ban the use of any and all crop and livestock protection chemicals. They are the antichemical group and the safety-at-any-cost people. They may not realize it but the cost is nothing short of less food, higher prices and eventual hunger. What will it profit a people to eliminate all substances that someone thinks might present a hazard when grossly misused, only to later find empty shelves at the supermarket? I am sure you will agree that this is not a sensible trade-off.

The conflict stems from divergent concepts held by most experienced toxicologists on the one hand and the safety-at-any-cost people on the other. The toxicologists using laboratory animals in dietary feeding studies and other tests determine the highest level of exposure that has no effect. Then to allow for possible differences between animals and man the professionals recommend maximum human exposures considerably below the proven no-effect level. It is based on these thorough investigations that government officials establish maximum safe daily intake levels and tolerances in food for those substances that may be present in traces.

The safety-at-any-cost people say that if there is any suspicion that a potential use of a chemical presents a hazard to man or the environment, then even traces should not be allowed. They hold to this view even though levels far above those that might be encountered have no effect on laboratory animals. Thus far their main emphasis has been on suspected carcinogens or cancer-inducing agents. The U.S. Food and Drug Law provides for the establishment of tolerances based on laboratory tests at various levels of exposure, except that if a compound shows the least evidence of inducing tumors in any strain of a laboratory animal, then according to present interpretation of the law, no tolerance can be established. It does not matter what route of administration is used or how exaggerated the dosage; any evidence of carcinogenicity is final.

It is highly probable that many if not most chemical compounds including natural components of the food we eat every day could be found to increase the incidence of tumors in one strain or another of laboratory mice if one tried various routes of administration with high dosages. The safety-at-any-cost people could probably discover the basis for demanding the banning of any useful flavoring or preservative or any crop or livestock protection chemical if they work hard enough at developing a more sensitive analytical method and conduct enough tests with laboratory animals for carcinogenicity. The antifood additive and antipesticide people are working diligently.

The paragraph in the U.S. Food and Drug Law which excludes suspected carcinogens from being eligible for tolerances in food is known as the Delaney Clause. Now effort is being made by the safety-at-any-cost people to extend the Delaney Clause philosophy to other effects such as teratogenesis, the occurrence of fetal defects. Here it is certain that many common substances would be found to be teratogenic or cause birth defects in laboratory animals if unnatural routes of exposure and ultra-high dosages were used. Common salt has been found to be teratogenic in one strain of laboratory mice in a Japanese laboratory and a U.S. Food and Drug Administration researcher has reported birth defects following the administration of high doses of vitamin A to test animals. These substances could hardly be banned, both being essential in the human diet. But that won't stop the antichemical people from trying to ban other substances, ones that may not be essential to your diet but very useful in insuring that you have enough food, enough that you can afford the luxury of dietary concerns.

Illnesses have occurred among farm workers who re-entered a field or orchard too soon after spraying with certain pesticides. Regulations governing re-entry times have long been needed and have now been set up in a number of countries. But again over-reaction seems to be the norm. Some regulations concerning the time that must elapse between application and re-entry for harvesting or other work appear to be in excess of need. If too wide a margin of safety is built into these regulations growers will be unable to manage certain pests and then get the crop harvested. One union now organizing agricultural workers in the United States, no doubt encouraged by the antichemical people, is demanding even wider margins of safety regarding re-entry times than set down by government standards. To add to the farmers confusion and discouragement, different departments within the U.S. Government have been feuding over the responsibility for establishing re-entry time regulations and administering them.

The new Federal Environmental Pesticide Control Act in the United States provides for a classification of pesticides according to the hazards associated with their use. After October 21, 1976, those designated as restricted may be applied only by certified applicators. The states which have the responsibility for training and certification have been slow to move, in part because at this writing they have not yet been told by the Environmental Protection Agency which chemicals and uses fall within the restricted category. Thus far neither federal nor state legislative bodies have appropriated funds needed for training hundreds of thousands of farmers and custom applicators. I am hopeful that the confusion will soon subside since further legislative or bureaucratic procrastination could jeopardize our food supply beginning in 1977.

The Far-Out Environmentalists

During the past decade, environmental protection has dominated man's concerns and his efforts. We are urged from all sides not to undertake new enterprises or modify our way of doing things without first considering all the consequences. What will a new product or a more efficient method do to the well-being of man and his environment? The ecologists urge us to take a "wholistic" approach.

Perhaps we are not really smart enough to perceive all the ultimate effects of changes, but certainly we will all agree that we should try. In my view, many environmentalists must also try harder. I believe they have been overlooking the probable detrimental effect of many of their actions and proposals on the greatest health need of all, a continuing supply of nutritious food. Many environmentalists seem to ignore the fact that people food is part of the environment, too.

A number of environmentalists have fallen prey to the myth that soil is exhausted by enriching its supply of essential mineral nutrients. In "A Blueprint For Survival," appearing in the British publication *Ecologist,* the authors refer to "damage to soil structure and long-term fertility" from the use of fertilizer. Barry Commoner in *The Closing Circle* refers to the "addiction" of soil to fertilizer nitrogen. Apparently mimicking Commoner's views, *Time Magazine* of February 2, 1970, stated, "Just as people get hooked on drugs, so the soil seems to be addicted to chemical additives and loses its ability to fix its own nitrogen." The most charitable thing a soil specialist could say about these statements is that they are grossly misleading. I will say they are completely erroneous or in a less charitable way, baloney! What are the facts?

Nitrogen is fixed by certain types of microorganisms, particularly those that live symbiotically on the roots of leguminous plants. When legume crops are fertilized liberally with a nitrogen fertilizer they may fix less atmospheric nitrogen than they would otherwise but there is no evidence that there is any lasting effect on the soil. It is the bacteria growing in nodules on the roots and not the soil itself that fixes nitrogen. In actual farm practice, leguminous crops are fertilized sparingly with nitrogen because of their special relationship to the nodule-forming bacteria.

The application of excess nitrogen fertilizer with subsequent runoff or leaching can contribute, along with sewerage and livestock effluent, to more rapid eutrophication of lakes or even present a human health hazard if excessive amounts reach ground water. But to condemn fertilizer per se instead of encouraging its wise use is like throwing out the baby with the bathwater. The conclusion of a National Academy of Sciences committee assigned to study nitrate accumulation in the environment indicates there is presently no widespread problem. They state in their 1972 report, ". . .the Committee finds no evidence of danger to man, animals or global environment from present patterns of fertilizer usage."

Far from exhausting a soil, fertilization with those mineral nutrients in which it is deficient gives it new life and leaves it in an improved nutritional and physical state. Well-nourished crops are big crops and the large amount of organic matter left behind after harvest, along with other sound management practices, makes today's good farmer a fertility builder. There has been much research progress toward fertilizer compositions that are less readily leached following heavy rain, as discussed in chapter 9. Between these developments and greater care in the timing of fertilizer applications the chances of nitrate leaching will be greatly reduced.

To err is human and apparently to overreact to errors of the past, particularly to other people's errors, is likewise human. A majority of past mistakes in the use of pesticides has been rectified by regulations together with the results of research on safer and more effective products. But the far-out environmentalists are still overreacting. Indeed, many appear determined to eliminate the use of crop and livestock protection chemicals entirely. Farmers, too, would like to produce your food without the use of chemicals since they cost money and require labor for application. But in spite of many useful genetic and biological controls, chemicals are still needed if the farmer is to survive economically and if you are to survive at all. Much research is underway on new approaches to pest control and the future may see the need for fewer chemicals, but that future is not yet here. Integrated controls in which pesticides play a less dominant part are proving to be successful in some farm situations but they are truly integrated and chemicals still play an important role. To the environmentalists, the term integrated control seems to be synonymous with eliminating chemicals altogether.

Let's continue our search for safer and more effective crop and livestock protection chemicals at the same time as we seek better genetic and biological methods of control. Then we can integrate all three to best advantage and if we are smart we will keep an alternate method in reserve in case of a failure. This happened with the biological screwworm control program in the United States in 1972. Suddenly there was an unexpected outbreak in the South and only because safe and effective insecticides were available did livestock growers avoid severe losses.

The environmentalist's complaint against monocultures stems in part from the sound ecological concept that a variety of plant types support a wider range of wildlife species. Actually, nature was not without her monocultures before man arrived, exemplified by the vast grasslands of central North America and Eurasia. Now we have large areas devoted mostly to wheat and barley and others to corn and soybeans. I agree that it would be desirable for us to have a wider range of food crops, but climatic limitations do not always permit it. In the nonirrigated prairies of western North America, what important food crop other than wheat can be profitably grown?

I also agree that it is desirable for each farm to have an area set aside for diversified vegetation in support of a range of wildlife species as discussed in chapter 5. But if cropland is properly managed to prevent erosion and build fertility, man's monocultures do not appear detrimental to our future. Alternate crops can be emphasized at any time the need arises providing fertility is maintained. The environmentalists and crop scientists agree, however, that genetic diversity within a species is highly desirable. Without it we may suddenly find vast acreages to be susceptible to a new disease.

The environmentalist's displeasure with monocultures is also associated with his or her notion that if a wider range of plants are grown pests will be less abundant. In an article in *Environment* of April, 1970, Barry Commoner referred to the desirability of ". . .a new, more mixed form of agriculture that will make it possible to get rid of most insecticides and make better use of the natural biological controls." Crop rotations do minimize some insects and diseases but others are little affected. There is little evidence that the need for man-managed control systems would be reduced by any practical level of diversification. The success we have had with biological controls did not come about by letting nature take its course in a mixed agriculture. Sterile male insect releases, bacterial diseases of insects and the culturing of predatory species all require a high level of technology and diligent attention to detail just as do the safe and successful uses of insecticides. Natural predators and parasites are very important to good insect management, and sound integrated control programs take every possible advantage of them through (1) the use of insecticides that are as selective as available, (2) proper timing of application, and (3) the use of the minimum dosage level needed to keep the pest population within reasonable limits. Just growing a lot of different crops and then letting nature take its course would be a sure road to food shortages.

We have a summer place in western Michigan with enough room for a small garden and a lone apple tree. The surrounding land is wild and includes a wood lot and brushy areas. There are no other gardens within a quarter mile. Some years the apples, which I never spray, are clean but in others they are riddled with maggots. I've tried growing cabbage and broccoli without an insecticide but the worms usually win even though there are no commercial plantings of these vegetables in the area. Farming in the region is highly diversified with deciduous fruit, canning beans, asparagus, field corn and alfalfa. These are well interspersed with unused land, woodlots, and pastures. In spite of this remarkable diversification I have been unable to see during the 30 years I have been spending holidays and weekends in the area that they have fewer pest problems than regions devoted to one or two crops. Growers have to be alert to outbreaks of asparagus beetle, and codling moth would soon put the apple producers out of business if they did not use controls. Fireblight of pears and cherry leaf spot are serious when weather conditions are right for these diseases. The area is about as far from being a monoculture as any food producing region I know of, but without diligent pest management the local farmers could make no more than a pitiful contribution to your food supply.

A final complaint about insecticides often heard from environmentalists is that insects develop resistance to them. This is true in many instances yet there is a remarkable lack of resistance to some compounds after dozens of generations. Genetic change is not confined to insects. Plant parasitic fungi develop resistance to the genetic factors that give certain varieties tolerance to specific diseases. Wheat resistant to stem rust is an example. No one condemns the concept of breeding for rust resistance. By diligent efforts the breeders have been able to keep ahead of the fungus and someday they may discover new genes for resistance that the disease cannot cope with.

Coccidia in poultry, which cause a universal disease that must be controlled by continuous feed medication, are constantly becoming resistant to the drugs in current use. Several effective anticoccidial drugs are available and by rotating them every few months permanent or high levels of resistance are avoided. Going back to insect pests, until alternate methods of control are available we must sometimes live with resistance by alternating compounds. The chances are good that new ones will be developed with the magic property of controlling a pest generation after generation without resistance appearing.

The Anti-Malthusians

Robert Malthus, the often maligned 18th century English clergyman-turned-economist, foresaw the clash of population with food supply nearly two centuries ago. However, he failed to visualize the great expansion in food production made possible by the development of new lands in the Americas and elsewhere. Needless to say, he had no way of anticipating our 20th century Yield Revolution. This faulty timing led many in recent years to say that Malthus was wrong. "Nothing to worry about! Look, he made these dire predictions a long time ago and we still have an abundance. Something will turn up, it always has!" Or will it? There is absolutely nothing on the horizon to suggest that food can keep pace for long with present rates of population growth being recorded in much of the world. Right now, and for a few years more, technology is buying us some time, but opportunities for yield increases are finite just as is the land available for agriculture. Some people, primarily in the prosperous industrialized countries, are using that time to bring their growth rates down while others are still reproducing at a terrific pace. In fact, many populations are growing faster than at any time in history as a result of continuing high birth rates on the one hand and public health programs on the other. In contrast to land and yield potential, man's capacity to reproduce is infinite.

Perhaps no one knows how lower birth rates in the presently fast growing, usually less developed, countries might be accomplished, but certainly those who say, "something will turn up, it always has," are not contributing to a solution. Nor are those who oppose birth control on moral or religious grounds. Where is the morality in contributing to a burgeoning population which at some point in its growth is certain to face dire food shortages? Those who discourage or even fail to encourage population control are among the Hunger Mongers.

It isn't clear just what effect the stand of the Roman Catholic church has on progress (or lack of it) toward reduced birth rates and eventually a population that the world can support indefinitely at a reasonable level of nutrition. If you look at the birth rates in some predominantly Catholic countries of Europe you may conclude that the church has little effect. But then look at Latin America and you have a different story. Births per 1000 population for some representative countries according to recent Population Reference Bureau estimates are as follows:

Brazil	38.0
Mexico	43.0
Colombia	45.0
U.S.A.	15.6
France	16.9
Italy	16.8
Spain	19.4

Regardless of your interpretation of these figures I think you will have to agree that in the predominantly Catholic countries of Latin America where food supply is perennially lagging behind needs, the current stand of the church is not helping bring birth rates down. It may be having a far more profound effect in encouraging a high birth rate than one might conclude from the European experience. I am hopeful that a change in the attitude of the church will remove it from the ranks of the Hunger Mongers.

And Others

There are other Hunger Mongers and at times most of us qualify in one way or another for the title, for example, when we waste food or consume more than needed for adequate nutrition. In the past, we smokers may have thought our habit was good for the agricultural economy but now there is no escaping the fact that tobacco requires land that might otherwise be devoted to food production. Beer and wine and other alcoholic beverages require much land for the grapes and various grains used in their production. Coffee and tea are not exempt. Hopefully a lowering of population growth rates together with improvement in agricultural production efficiency will not make it necessary for us to choose between life's amenities and basic food requirements. But if a food supply crisis ever develops, let's not ignore the facts.

If a real food crunch ever comes our luxury diets, wasted food and amenities we smoke or drink are not the only demands on dwindling land resources that will have to be modified. More than fifty million cats and dogs plus an estimated seven million nonfarm horses in the United States require more than ten million acres of land for their support. Fertilizer shortages may continue to limit food production in the decades ahead as they now do in some less industrialized countries. Perhaps an adequate lawn can be maintained with less feeding than now commonly practiced. There is always the possibility of recycling the fertilizer we apply to our grass by using the clippings as a mulch for fruit or vegetable plantings.

I hesitate to say unkind words about the press, radio and television. Having once been involved in the seed business and later in the agricultural chemical business, where a new variety or a new crop protection product takes years after initial discovery to reach the marketplace, I have deep-felt admiration for anyone who puts out a new product every day or even every week or month. Nonetheless, the media contribute at times to the lack of public confidence in our food supply and thereby to overregulation. It appears easy to write scare headlines about poisons in our food, the natural environment being ruined or a pesticide killing some fish. You have seen or heard these one-sided stories and will again. A check point for accuracy of an agriculturally related story is as close as a reporter's phone. A call to the Agricultural Experiment Station or Extension Director at any university having an agricultural college will bring referral to a specialist.

The professional agricultural societies of the United States recently organized the Council for Agricultural Science and Technology (CAST) for the purpose of providing scientific and technical information on any phase of agriculture as requested by Congress, governmental agencies or the media. By making a call to the CAST office at Ames, Iowa (515-294-2036), a reporter can obtain the names of top authorities in any phase of agriculture.

Even writers without tight deadlines seem to shun verification when writing about things far from their area of expertise. I am an admirer of Peter Drucker and his writings on business management. But I wish he had taken time to learn what has been going on in pesticide laboratories during the last few years before he wrote the article, "Saving the Crusade," in *Harpers* for January, 1972. In discussing the need to balance environmental risks with economic realities he stated:

> Today, for example, no safe pesticides exist, nor are any in sight. We may ban DDT, but all the substitutes so far developed have highly undesirable properties. Yet if we try to do without pesticides altogether, we shall invite massive hazards of disease and starvation the world over.

Mr. Drucker has apparently never taken the time to learn about the many insecticides that, with a modicum of care in following label directions, are safe to both people and the environment. Malathion, Ronnel, Abate, Plictran, Methoxychlor, Dursban, Sumithion are insecticides for specific uses as directed on their government approved labels. They hardly have "highly undesirable properties," unless you consider a hazard from gross misuse as highly undesirable, misuse in a class with driving a car down the road at 100 mph or swallowing the compound intended for your dishwasher. Each of these new insecticides and indeed many others in its own way has overcome some of the ecological problems some people have attributed to DDT.

There are also the overresponsive lawmakers looking for a popular cause. The far-out environmentalists and safety-at-any-cost people have often found attentive ears in the legislative halls of many countries. At times regulatory laws have indeed been needed, but there is a difference between a problem and a crisis. Too often new laws have been enacted in a crisis atmosphere created for the occasion. Those responsible for detailed interpretation and the administration of the pesticide laws are, on the whole, dedicated people with the overall public good at heart. But they are under constant pressure from the antichemical cult who urge more rigid control often far beyond those needed for public protection.

The high costs of making a new crop protection chemical available that inevitably result from picayunish registration requirements have already discouraged the search for safer and more effective compounds. Your future supply of fruits and vegetables at a price you can afford is in particular jeopardy. All added together, the acreage of these specialty foods that supply us with minerals and vitamins and add zest to our meals totals only about one percent of the area devoted to crops. This small percentage is made up of dozens of species, so there is difficulty in justifying the research needed to obtain registration of a pesticide for just one of them. There is no way a grower can make a viable enterprise of producing fruits and vegetables without controlling fungus diseases, mites, nematodes and many insect pests. Crop protection chemicals are often needed. If we regulate present pesticides out of existence and then make the search for safer and more effective ones unprofitable, our lettuce, tomatoes, peaches and dozens of other fruits and vegetables that help make life worth living may become very expensive luxuries or just fond memories. Of course our fruits and vegetables must be safe to eat, but the price of demanding investigations far beyond those needed to insure human protection will most certainly be a dwindling supply of these health-giving foods.

Among the Hunger Mongers are the careless, the selfish and the ignorant who misuse pesticides by not following the directions and precautions on the label. Those words were printed there after extensive and expensive research. They constitute compromises and agreement among scientists and regulatory officials of many specialities as to what is effective and what is safe. Margins of safety are built into label directions, but to deviate from them is not only a violation of the law but a contribution to the antichemical cause. Every farmer must remember that he can carelessly use his tractor on the highway and kill some people and there will only be a short column in the local paper reporting the incident. But if he carelessly lets some surplus insecticidal spray drain into a stream and kill a few fish, he can really make headlines.

The authors of the book "Hard Tomatoes, Hard Times" were very critical of publicly supported Agricultural Experiment

Stations because, in their view, the new technology coming from those institutions only benefits the more successful farmers and does little for the rural poor. In my view the work of these stations has benefited all of us.   I shudder to think what our food picture would have been like since 1972 had they not long ago provided us with rust resistant wheats.   Bread rationing would have become a reality.   Practically every basic food is more abundant because of publicly supported research.   True, the underfinanced and technically less competent farmer has not benefited to the fullest extent but this is a social and educational problem yet to be solved.   To divert continuing research aimed at making food production more efficient would invite scarcity for our children and later generations.   The rural poor and the marginal farmer are not the primary producers of the tremendous volumes required to keep market shelves well-stocked. They do need help but let's give it to them through appropriate social and educational programs.

Not all the Hunger Mongers will go away.   Chances are some will be with us for a long time.   Even countries currently short of food have their share.   Let's not contribute to their efforts, unwittingly or otherwise.   Let's not let them undermine our ability to produce food in abundance so our market shelves will always be filled.

Much public land in the western United States can be wisely managed for multiple uses; grazing, forest tree production and recreation. Here cattle graze in summer at a high altitude in the Gravely Range in Montana.

7

The Great Protein War

Recent price increases have awakened us to the fact of life that meat is a luxury. Animal protein is nutritious of course, and pleasant to consume. There is no escaping the fact, however, that in terms of the land and labor resources required to put them in the supermarket, meat and eggs are definitely a luxury and dairy products are not far behind. Now don't get me wrong, I am far from a vegetarian. There is nothing I like better than bacon and eggs for breakfast, a juicy hamburger with a glass of milk for lunch and perhaps chicken or a roast for my evening meal. But if I eat that much animal protein in one day I am exceeding the amount needed for good nutrition and demanding a disproportionate share of the earth's food production capacity, not to mention the strain on my wife's food budget.

With the exception of short periods, chiefly during wartime, people in the New World have had cheap meat. First it was wild game and then beef from range animals that cost little to raise. Farm-produced animals have dominated our meat supply for many decades, but during that period we had cheap land for pasture and inexpensive feed grains. Now world-wide demand for grain has caught up with supply and the farmer, who with few exceptions didn't make what the majority of us would consider a decent living during most of the past 25 years, is beginning to get a better return for his labors.   But more expensive land, more costly grain for feed and a better labor return to the farmer are only a part of the increases in the cost of producing meat. If you are employed in the steel, paper or chemical industries and are making more money than you were two years ago, you have played a part in the price increase. If you have anything to do with trucks, tractors, petroleum, packages or electric power and have had a raise you also had a part in rising meat prices. The farmer, producing meat, eggs or milk and also the feed which his animals consume, must have tractors, motor fuel, fencing, silos, fertilizer and pesticides. Then, in order to change the farmer's products to the sausage, cheese, ice cream, milk, eggs and meat cuts you put in your shopping basket, the transportation and food-processing people need equipment, energy, packages and lots of labor seeking higher pay.

Regardless of your source of income, if you, like many people of the world, are using a part of any increase in take-home pay to purchase more livestock products, you are partly responsible for higher prices. An increase in demand for meat, milk and eggs not only increases prices of these foods but also grains and everything made from them.   After all pigs and poultry eat grain; lots of it. It takes several pounds of grain to produce a pound of pork or chicken. Much beef is fed entirely on grass but if you buy one of the higher grades it probably came from an animal finished on grain.   So if you buy a fair sized roast for dinner it actually means that you are purchasing close to a bushel of corn or its equivalent in other feeds.   With a 50 pound per capita increase in meat consumption in the United States during the last 20 years together with an increase in demand from abroad it's no wonder that grain reserves are down and prices are up.

Livestock and Human Nutrition

Let's make it doubly clear why meat is a luxury because only with this understanding can you comprehend the protein war that is being waged in the world today and the tough decisions we will have to make in the future.

First a mother animal has to be raised to the reproductive stage and then cared for while she is producing the piglets, calves or chicks that will be grown on for meat, milk or egg production. This phase of agriculture is fairly efficient with poultry. One mother hen will produce over 20 dozen hatching eggs in a year. Pigs are next in efficiency. Two litters a year of a dozen piglets each are not uncommon. But the most inefficient of all is the cow which must be raised and fed for two full years before she produces her first calf and then takes a full year before she produces another. Considering losses, brood cows average only about eight-tenths of a calf per year to raise on to slaughter size. There is a lot of money per pound tied up in a beef animal the day it is born.

Poultry and hogs require grain or other expensive concentrated feeds. As meat animals, cattle are not very efficient converters requiring more calories and more protein to produce a pound of human food than some other species, but their saving grace is that they can eat grass and other roughages and therefore cost less to feed than if they had to have concentrates throughout their life. Thus the inefficiency of cattle from the reproductive standpoint is partially made up by the fact that they can graze and consume plants often grown on poor soil ill-adapted to crop production. But cattle and also sheep, the other important species that can digest roughages, still require a lot of land, and cheap land seems to be a thing of the past.

Actually, many cattle grown for meat in North America are fattened or finished on grain during the last few months of their life in order to get more tender steaks and roasts. The meat from such animals carries more fat, a factor in tenderness and flavor but an expensive form of calories. When grain was cheap this was not an unreasonable procedure economically speaking, but we may be approaching the time when North Americans will have to be content with more grass-fed beef as people now are in much of the meat-eating world. There is nothing wrong with beef from animals that have consumed only hay and pasture forage plus minerals and nonprotein nitrogen supplements. The excellently flavored beef I've eaten in Argentina had less fat than that ordinarily found at your supermarket (certainly a nutritional plus) but you do need a sharp knife or a tenderizer. Much of the lean grass-fed beef we import from Australia and other countries is processed into hamburger, particularly for fast-food outlets.

There is a middle way between the long finishing period as practiced in recent years in North America and the strictly grass-fed beef of the rest of the world. Carrying animals on grass until they have reached three-quarters or more of their eventual market weight, instead of only 50 to 60 percent as has been recently practiced, can give a good quality carcass at a lower cost if pastures are managed efficiently and rainfall is adequate. At the same time, reducing the period in the feedlot minimizes the amount of manure that has to be disposed of. Economically and nutritionally, corn or grass silage is very favorable for finishing beef animals. Although most silage is really a crop and requires land adapted to mechanical farming operations, it can be produced under a far wider range of climatic conditions than grain. Many feed lots are now using a ration that includes considerable silage in addition to grain.

Nutritionally speaking, we eat meat, milk and eggs for their protein content and these products have special merit because the essential amino acids, the building blocks of complex protein molecules, are present in the right proportion to fit man's needs. Actually, these same amino acids make up the protein in cereals and other foods of plant origin but seldom in the right proportion in a single species. People who eat little meat, milk or eggs and obtain their protein from plant sources can get along fine if their amino acid intake is balanced by having foods derived from different species. Protein in wheat, rice and corn is low in one of the key amino acids, lysine, but well supplied with another important one, methionine. Beans, soybeans and some other edible legumes are the reverse, being rich in lysine and low in methionine. A diet of beans and corn in Latin America or legumes with rice in Asia are food combinations that enable tens of millions to maintain health with few animal products in their diet, providing of course that they have enough of these to eat.

Actually poultry and hogs, both species with a single stomach like man, are merely converters of concentrated plant protein to animal protein, and they must also be fed a balanced ration for efficient growth. Hence, the importance of soybean meal with corn in preparing mixed feeds. Synthetic methionine is also used in balancing poultry rations to get the most efficient production. Hog rations based largely on corn are often balanced with lysine. In the process of conversion the animal uses much of its feed to maintain body heat and to produce inedible skin, feathers and bone. We end up with a few ounces of high-moisture lean meat on our plate which took pounds of dry feed to produce.

Cattle, sheep and other ruminants have a different kind of digestive system than hogs or poultry. Their rumen is a large fermentation vat through which food passes enroute to their stomach, where masticated grass and hay are fermented by bacteria which synthesize essential amino acids. Thus we don't have to be so concerned about feeding balanced proteins to ruminants which, in fact, can utilize nonprotein sources of nitrogen such as urea or biuret. The rumen bacteria build protein using such sources of nitrogen plus minerals and energy derived from other foods.

But no matter how much we improve the efficiency of animal agriculture the output in edible protein, the muscle tissue we actually eat without counting all the waste, will always be but a fraction of the animal's protein intake. This doesn't mean we should not strive for more efficient conversion, but to understand the question of grain versus meat, we have to recognize that it takes feed to make hide, bone, hair, feathers and the organs that find little use as human food.

Dairy cattle, at least high producing ones, are more efficient converters of plant protein to human food than beef animals. Not counting the protein needed for initial growth and maintenance during and between the lactation periods, a good cow can yield milk carrying two-thirds as much protein as she consumes. But, of course, she has to be grown in the first place and like any adult animal requires some protein to maintain body tissues. On the plus side of the ledger, dairy animals produce a calf for each lactation period which has considerable replacement value for milk production or as an animal to raise on for beef. When you add all these up, a high producing milk cow which can digest a lot of roughage as well as grain is certainly the most efficient converter of plant protein to animal protein that man has domesticated. This is reflected in the cost of actual protein in milk as compared with that in lean meat. For example, with 3.3 percent protein in low-fat milk at 35 cents a quart (which weighs a little over two pounds), the cost of actual protein is about $5.00 per pound. On the other hand, the cost of protein in boneless lean meat at $1.50 per pound is over $8.00 per pound of protein equivalent. Of course, any bone or fat in the meat you buy doesn't contribute to protein nutrition. Powdered milk and also products made from milk, for example cottage cheese at 19 percent protein, are often the most economical animal source of this essential food component.

The laying hen is also a fairly efficient converter if she is producing a large number of eggs, thus spreading the rearing and maintenance ration costs over, say 20 dozen or more a year. A low producing hen on the other hand, like a low producing milk cow, is a drain on resources. It takes as much feed for initial rearing and body maintenance of a poor producer as it does an outstanding one. Think of the cow or a hen as a factory. It costs as much to build and takes as much to heat a factory producing only limited goods as it does another of a similar size where all the wheels are turning. The goods produced depend on the design of the machinery (the genetic capacity in the case of a bird or an animal), but also on keeping the right mix and volume of raw materials flowing into the hopper. Just as good maintenance is important to a manufacturing plant's productivity, good care including parasite and disease control is of utmost importance to the success of a milk or egg "factory."

No matter how much we can improve the efficiency of poultry or livestock, the protein derived from them will always be more expensive than from plant sources. Compare the protein equivalents mentioned above at current costs with wheat flour at 10 percent protein, rice at 7.5 percent, corn meal at 9 percent and dry peas and beans at more than 20 percent. It is easy to see why soybeans are such an important source of protein for feeds and processed foods when you consider that they contain about 36 percent protein, and at the same time are a rich source of oil suitable for margarine and cooking oil preparations.

Protein Nutrition in the Other World

Healthy people in some of the poorer parts of Asia and Latin America who eat very little protein of animal origin give evidence that with the proper balance of cereals supplemented by vegetables and fruits, good nutrition can be achieved without meat, eggs or dairy products. Dry legumes including beans, lentils and chickpeas figure prominently in the diet of these people. Rice in the Orient and corn in addition to rice in Latin America are the prime sources of calories. Both of these grains have appreciable protein although low in the essential amino acid lysine. A dietary blend with the higher lysine legumes makes a reasonably well balanced diet, providing of course, that there is enough of this food assortment throughout the year. If one has to rely on low protein plant products for their entire source it is essential to keep daily intake at a high level even though not all the carbohydrate that comes in the same kernel of corn or grain of rice may be needed.

The great nutritional problem of the world is not the meat-less people who get a balance of cereals and legumes, but the tens of millions, particularly in tropical countries, who survive on low protein cassava root and grain sorghum. They may have enough calories derived from these starchy foods but protein is definitely lacking in their diet. Yams and bananas and other products of subsistence gardening in the tropics cannot make up the deficiency. Of course, many do not have enough to eat. They are deficient in calories to furnish the energy for body functions as well as protein for tissue building.

Whether the problem is imbalance or simply hunger, it is the children who are affected most pathetically. Adults must have enough protein for tissue replacement but children and youth need larger amounts in their diet to nourish growing tissues. It is now recognized that severe protein deficiency in children can impair their mental as well as physical development. Some cultures seem caught up in a vicious cycle in which there is not enough protein for physical and mental vigor and little chance of improving their lot without these attributes. The period of greatest hazard is immediately after weaning. The child may have gotten along very well on its mother's milk, possibly at the expense of her nutrition, but the foods available after weaning are often just not adequate in quality even though the quantity is enough. Children under three or four cannot handle the bulk in diets that derive all their protein from cereals, root crops, plantain and other food plants. The pot-bellies of children one sees among very poor and ill-fed people are a symptom of marked protein deficiency, a condition called Kwashiorkor. It is most likely to occur following a respiratory or enteric infection, both common among the poorly nourished. Again another vicious circle.

I had read about Kwashiorkor, of course, but my first glimpse of a community-wide occurrence of this deficiency disease came several years ago in the Dominican Republic. With a business associate, I had been inspecting pastures treated with a new herbicide for controlling the thickets of brush that keep so much of the Caribbean from producing much milk or meat. On the return to Santo Domingo we took a side trip up into some beautiful mountains and I could not help but envy the people living in the tiny dwellings on those peaceful slopes. Judging from their plots of cassava, yam and plaintain along with other tropical fruits and vegetables, their soil was reasonably fertile and rainfall adequate for subsistence gardening.

Then we went a little higher and the narrow and rutted road began to follow a rushing stream that came tumbling down its rocky course overhung with tree ferns and other lush tropical vegetation. Beyond, on a relatively moderate slope, we could see other dwellings. I first thought that this was an idyllic place in which to live with year-round warm weather yet high enough to avoid the stifling heat of the lowlands. There was plenty of rain without the long dry season of some parts of the island and cultivated plots indicated at least a fair level of soil fertility.

Then I saw the children. Most of them had the typical pot-bellied appearance of severe protein deficiency one sees pictured in press reports of famine. They seemed listless compared with the kids I had passed in the village near the cattle ranch that morning. A look at their hillside plots indicated why there could be a protein deficiency here in these beautiful surroundings. There was a dominance of cassava, often called manioc, the low protein, starchy root crop so many millions in the tropics survive on. There was little corn and I saw no evidence of upland rice. No doubt insects and grain-eating birds made these cereals almost impossible to grow. Assorted tropical fruits and vegetables made up the balance of the food gardens but there were none that could make up for the low protein content of cassava. I caught sight of a couple of goats and one pig but obviously the hundred or so people isolated in this tropical mountain community had little animal protein in their diet. Yet, a thriving and expanding cattle operation was only 50 miles away, a venture that had fine commercial prospects for the future because of the ever-increasing demand for beef in Puerto Rico just across the Mona Passage.

The world seems to be engaged in a great protein war in which affluent people strive to get more because high protein foods are good to eat, and the poor fight just to get enough for decent health. There is no argument over protein foods being good for you. When consumed in larger amounts than required for minimum nutrition, they serve as a safety reserve. They furnish energy when eaten in excess of nutritional needs but at a much higher cost than carbohydrate foods. The wide publicity given high protein reducing diets has contributed to a worship of lean meat and other protein foods. Protein is by far the most expensive of our food components and as one might expect, the more affluent are winning the war. Tremendous amounts of meat and fish are shipped from the poorer countries where millions are malnourished. Tens of millions of pets in the more affluent parts of the world get more protein each day than required for the best of nutritional health by a growing child or a physically active adult.

Sooner or later the moral question of the more affluent countries importing so much protein from ill-fed nations will have to be answered. I am not talking about the huge importation of meat from Australia where raising beef for export is their business. Australians are hardly ill-nourished. But how about the importation of meat and fish from poor countries, much of whose populations do not get enough protein for a healthy life? These are the countries where so many children are protein starved after weaning and as a result may be permanently impaired in their mental development. We have dabbled at technical assistance in helping them produce more edible legumes and we have sent them breeding stock of high lysine corn which could be of material help in supplying protein with a desirable amino acid balance if it came into wide use. But these aid programs are little more than tokens in relation to the need.

If an affluent country imports protein foods or feed from areas whose people are malnourished, I believe more intensive technical and financial aid should be given, possibly supported by an earmarked import duty. There is nothing wrong with importing expensive protein foods such as shrimp or beef from Central America if their people have enough less expensive protein for good health. But they often do not, and importing countries should do something about it through research and development on lower cost sources, distribution of seeds and the promotion of local food processing industries.

Although the more affluent countries have seen some reduction in meat consumption since prices increased, the spread in protein intake between the haves and the havenots is still tremendous. Perhaps marked dietary changes in the affluent segment of society are too much to expect, but significant increases in protein food production at a more rapid rate than population growth is quite possible if enough research and development effort is pointed in that direction. Of course, if a growing proportion of people have the money to demand more than their share we would still have protein rich and protein poor worlds with a great dietary gulf between. But certainly without greater production there is little chance the lot of the poorly nourished will improve.

Can Protein Supplies be Increased

How can we continue to have a reasonable amount of animal protein in our diet? Can new sources be found that will give today's ill-nourished people a better chance of getting enough protein, whatever its origin? One phase of the protein war is being waged on the technical front, by agriculturists, food technologists and others striving to develop new and better ways to produce protein foods for all the world. Here are the new and improved sources of protein on the horizon.

Beef. There are vast opportunities in many parts of the world to materially increase the production of grass-fed beef. Much land unfit for cropping is badly infested with unpalatable or nonnutritious brush and economic methods are now available and being used for its elimination. Fertilizer is often needed. If the outstanding pasture improvements I have seen here and there around the world become widespread, the carrying capacity of land now devoted to livestock could be greatly increased, perhaps doubled. Given proper care with modern veterinary products for insects and other parasites, cattle of one breed or another can be grown in most places where vegetation will thrive. There have been a number of publicly funded foreign aid programs related to increased beef production on land not adapted to crops. These should be intensified. Possibly there would then be enough for export for needed foreign exchange and still some left over so people in the producing country could eat beef more frequently. Commercial development programs related to improvement of grazing land and better livestock health have also made significant contributions to meat production in many parts of the world. These will certainly be expanded if the countries with land resources for more extensive and improved cattle raising maintain a political climate that can make agribusiness profitable.

Even in the United States there are significant opportunities for expanded beef production. Larger supplies are not needed at the time of this writing in 1975. Beef is actually in surplus, largely due to reduced buying power and lower demand. But looking ahead, beef production can be greatly expanded if the economy dictates.

I have traveled extensively in the eastern United States in the last few years in areas where crop acreage is down. You see intensive cattle production in parts of Virginia and Kentucky but on the whole our land east of the great mid-continent cropping areas and north of the Gulf States is under-utilized. Much is best adapted to forests and, of course, we want some in a wild state. But productive pastures interspersed with blocks of trees give the "edge effect" so many wildlife species seem to favor. Ecologically as well as economically I see no reason why there should not be an expansion in eastern cattle enterprises. If only pastures and not feed lots are involved, they don't have to stay far away from settled areas. Grazing cattle on a green hillside can be an aesthetic asset for any suburban community.

Dairy Products.   There is a potential for a protein rich spinoff from improved beef operations in the less developed countries even though the bulk of the meat may be exported. Once farmers in an area learn the latest technology involved in maintaining productive pastures and protecting the health of their livestock, it is not too big a jump into an efficient dairy business. Probably climatic conditions prevent dairying from ever being quite as efficient in the tropics as it is in the North. But the dairy cow is still a wonder at converting protein from plant material inedible by man to milk and from that to cheese, both excellent protein foods with the right amino acid balance for people. I've watched the outstanding dairy development in Puerto Rico with much interest in recent years, perhaps because I saw that island's almost complete lack of improved dairy cattle on my first trip there in 1934. Pangola grass, better protection against parasites, and superior breeding stock have converted the island from an importer to a condition of self-sufficiency with respect to dairy products.

Fish.   Seafood comes up in any conversation regarding increased protein for the world's burgeoning population. Catches of "wild fish" are believed by many specialists to have reached a leveling off point. The failure of the Peruvian anchovy industry in 1972 and 1973 raises serious questions regarding our ability to sustain the catches we had in the 1960's. Recently the catch of North Atlantic species has fallen off. Even the more optimistic fishery specialists now predict that the world fish take can sustain a percentage growth no more than equal to population, and this for only a few more years. Oceans, like land, are finite and the sustained catch of "wild" fish cannot exceed the carrying capacity of the waters they inhabit. Attempts to regulate ocean fishing in interests of maximum sustained catches have fallen short of needs. Here is a real challenge to international co-operation. If edible fish catches fall off, countries like Japan and Russia, whose people now get a significant portion of their protein from fish, are likely to be in the market for more meat or feed grains. Their people have the expectation of having frequent meals that include food of animal origin.

A very sizable part of the world's fish catch is processed into meal used in livestock feed. Methods are now available for preparing a low cost edible protein-rich "flour" from aquatic species that are considered poorly adapted to direct human consumption. Some not now widely harvested, for example, the Antarctic Krill, are believed to be available in tremendous quantities. If these processes become widespread and the product is accepted for fortifying other foods, it could contribute much to better nutrition. Incidentally, the poor catch of fish for meal production off Peru in 1972 contributed significantly to increased demand for soybean meal, an alternate source of protein for poultry and livestock. As much as anything else, this triggered the increasing prices of meat and other foods.

Cultured Aquatic Life. Farming the oceans has been a popular subject for those who like to predict the world of the future. There have been successes with oysters, particularly in Japan, and promising results with other shellfish. Raising swimming salt water fish in cages suspended in the water is being done on a pilot scale in Scotland. No doubt many of these schemes will prove successful, but one has to remember that fish must eat as regularly as a pig or a chicken if they are to grow rapidly. Unless given supplemental feed, their numbers cannot exceed the carrying capacity of the water surrounding them. The capital required for most fish growing schemes is very high and disease problems are sometimes overwhelming. Domesticated animals suffered severe and often catastrophic losses from insects, helminth parasites and various diseases from the beginning of agriculture until very recent years. A tremendous amount of research went into our modern systems of livestock and poultry health protection. Similar research on fish diseases and parasites is still in its infancy.

Culturing freshwater fish in ponds, in raceways and in cages suspended in flowing water is practiced in many parts of the world. Carp and milk fish are preferred species in Asia, carp in Europe and trout and catfish in the United States. The White Amur, sometimes called the grass carp, has interesting possibilities because it can digest vegetable matter. But these captive fish must all be fed and the food for the most part comes from the land. A large mill devoted to making pelleted catfish food in Mississippi uses a formula not greatly different from that of a neighboring mill specializing in poultry feed. Soybean meal is the chief source of protein and fish are theoretically the most efficient converters of all because they do not expend energy maintaining a constant high body temperature. But there are a lot of problems connected with their commercial production in concentrated numbers. I look for fish culture to expand, but not in the quantum jump needed to solve our problems of protein shortage.

Of all the new food productions schemes that have received wide publicity in advance of proof of technical and economic practicality, the various algae culture experiments take the prize. Perhaps you recall those news releases in the 1950s. Algae have the advantage of being green plants and carrying on photosynthesis. Thus they were visualized as being a new primary source of food and feed. Small-scaled experiments indicated the possibilities of fabulous yields of protein, fats and other food elements, and various schemes were tried out for containing the algae, usually of a unicellular type. Tanks and vats and other containers designed to make the greatest use of solar energy were visualized. Some research on algae culture is still underway and I think something practical may come of it, but so far the economics look less favorable than for conventional farm crops. Capital requirements for an operation of any size are overwhelming and problems of disease and competing aquatic organisms horrendous. For the immediate future I suspect we will have to be content with water chestnut and seaweed as eaten in Japan and Korea as our main source of edible aquatic plants.

Protein from Microorganisms.   Bacteria, yeasts and fungi cannot utilize the sun's energy to carry on photosynthesis. But if we supply them with carbohydrate made earlier by a green plant or some other form of "fixed" carbon as a source of energy, along with inorganic nutrients, these lower organisms can then synthesize amino acids and from them proteins. This is what takes place in the cow's rumen, a large pouch that holds masticated food before it reaches the true stomach. It is in this living fermentation vat that bacteria digest roughages and form the protein that makes up much of their cellular contents. The cow then digests the bacteria as they pass through the rest of the animal's digestive tract.

Bacteria, yeasts and some fungi can also grow and therefore synthesize protein in a man-made vat if given the proper feed stock. It may be an agricultural waste or a by-product such as molasses, or it can even be certain hydrocarbon fractions of petroleum along with essential minerals. Yeast has also been produced on certain papermill wastes.

So what are we waiting for? Why not use petroleum and all the agricultural and forestry wastes in the world to produce cheap protein for livestock feed, if not for human consumption? Actually, a lot of progress has been made. There are pilot plants in operation in France and England producing bacterial protein using a petroleum fraction as a substrate.

During war time food shortages in Scandinavia, the cellulose in wood was reduced to a simpler carbohydrate by acid treatment, and yeast for human or livestock consumption then grown on the resulting broth. Recent research points up the possibility of using *Cellulomonas,* a kind of bacteria that can grow directly on cellulose. Currently a pilot plant at Louisiana State University is employing a selected strain of this bacterium for the production of feed-grade protein from sugar cane bagasse.

All these things can be done, but we are only on the threshold of learning how to carry out the processes efficiently. The microbiologist and the chemical engineer have only in recent years teamed up to learn best how to "farm" these lower forms of plants to produce food for people or animals. Research and development in this area has been rather meagerly supported considering the magnitude of the world's food problems. I think more effort by our best brains should be committed to this kind of technology.

Extracting Protein. It is truly sad that a number of countries whose people have too little protein to eat actually have so much of plant origin that might be used with a little more technical development. When you think of the peanut as a crop, the roasted and salted product we eat at the ballgame no doubt comes to mind, and, of course, there is the ever-favorite peanut butter. It usually comes as a surprise to North Americans that groundnuts, as peanuts are called in most parts of the world, are primarily raised for the cooking oil that is extracted from them. Large acreages are grown in India and in West Africa. Much of the meal remaining after extracting the oil is not used for food or feed but goes back into the ground for its fertilizer value. This is in sharp contrast to the soybean, the world's leading oil crop, which is also at the same time the world's leading source of protein concentrate. Using soybean meal or cotton seed meal for fertilizer in this day and age would be unthinkable since the protein these meals carry is so valuable as food or feed and chemical fertilizer is cheaper in terms of equivalent plant nutrient value.

The idea of using seed meals as fertilizer goes back to the days before our chemists learned how to "fix" the nitrogen from the air with hydrogen to make ammonia fertilizer. But why have seed meals continued to be applied to the land when a protein extract from them could be so useful as food? Aphlatoxin, a poison that comes from a fungus that attacks peanuts if improperly dried, is a part of the answer, but this toxin can now be identified in stored nuts and prevented by proper handling. A peanut protein-isolate process was on the verge of becoming commercial in India a few years ago but delays in approval by the Indian government caused the capital ready to build a plant to find another home.

For some reason, governments seem overly cautious whenever a new protein food is proposed. The U.S. Food and Drug Administration dragged its feet for years before giving partial approval to fish flour, usually made from species now used only for fish meal for animal feeding. Recently Japanese petroleum and chemical companies halted some promising microbial protein research and development because their government was insisting on picayunish investigations of safety far in excess of the toxicological tests most scientists thought adequate for public protection. This is another case of the safety-at-any-cost people dominating governmental policy even if it means that someone will be malnourished as a result.

Considerable research is currently underway on techniques of extracting protein from leaves. People have been asking, why not extract the protein for human food and bypass the animal? No doubt schemes like this will eventually become practical. The total protein produced in, say, a crop of alfalfa is far above that which can be obtained when the same alfalfa is fed to meat animals and significantly greater than if converted to milk. Leaf-protein isolates can be useful not only for poultry and livestock but also for fortifying common foods such as bread or used as a component of synthetic milk. Recent work at the University of Nebraska points up the acceptability of a range of foods fortified with an alfalfa protein-isolate. Alfalfa gives an outstanding yield of protein in temperate or arid regions where it can be grown. However, other plants must be investigated for the humid tropics where so much of the world's protein deficiency occurs and the need for a cheap fortifying agent is greatest. In recent research in India, Napier grass, a giant tropical species, has been found promising for protein extraction.

New Crops and New Livestock Species.   The number of plant or animal species that have been domesticated during the last ten thousand years is surprisingly small. Were our ancestors who first began to take care of animals and later settled down in one spot and cultivated plants so intelligent that they picked out all the best candidates for agricultural and genetic development? I suspect they were not that smart. Perhaps we have been so preoccupied with improving the crop and livestock species handed down to us that we are overlooking some other good bets, ones that could help with our protein problem. Just recently in an article in *World Crops,* a horticulturist from Ghana told of experiments with three tropical leafy vegetables all of which had five percent protein based on their fresh weight. This is higher than the protein level of most of our leafy garden vegetables such as lettuce and cabbage. A report from Australia points out the high lysine content of a grain-type Amaranthus (related to pigweed) thought to be common in Central America prior to the Spanish conquest and currently important in some of the mountainous regions of northern India. Such a grain could be a valuable adjunct to cereals low in this essential amino acid. I think more of this type of exploration of little-cultivated and even wild plants should be conducted.

You may have read of recent experiments with the Musk Ox, an Arctic species that can survive very severe conditions. We have to remember that Arctic ranges cannot carry a very high population of any large animal, but the musk ox, along with reindeer, may add to the food producing capacity of the far North. The much publicized Beefalo, a hybrid between the American bison and cattle, may provide another hardier range animal for rigorous climates. Like cattle, these and other large animals have reproductive limitations so they can hardly offer an opportunity for a spectacular reduction in the cost of meat, but they could add significantly to total supply.

Many students of the large animals of Africa believe that certain ones, for example, the eland, would adapt well to domestication. If species resistant to the Tsetse fly, which makes cattle growing in some areas most difficult, could be domesticated, it could have tremendous benefit to people who are now experiencing a severe shortage of protein in their diet. An additional advantage is that some presently wild animals graze readily on plant species that are rejected by cattle. Rotational grazing if not actual joint grazing by two species may be a way to increase pasture yield providing it is not overdone to the extent that erosion is induced. Water Buffalo, a ruminant common in the orient as a beast of burden, is also a source of milk and meat. It withstands the rigors of the tropics better than most cattle and should be investigated further as a primary food source in areas now short of protein.

Actually, we long ago domesticated animals that have slipped in favor in many places but which may stage a comeback. Sheep, still the dominant ruminant animal in some parts of the world, are better adapted than cattle to very rough country and may again become important in parts of North America. The goat has a prominent place in history, partly because it denuded so much land, particularly in the Mediterranean Basin where pastures were overgrazed and erosion became rampant. Sheep and goats eat close to the ground and special care must be exercised in managing grazing areas for those animals. Recent range management investigations in the Western United States indicate that the yield of meat per unit area of land can sometimes be increased by rotational or even joint grazing of sheep or goats with cattle.

The rabbit is a meat animal widely used in Europe and one that North Americans would do well to get better acquainted with. I raised them as a boy and I well recall their utility in converting many kitchen scraps such as peelings, vegetable tops, stale bread, etc., to delicious meat. We raised a large garden and stored potatoes, cabbage, carrots and other root crops, and the rabbits were always glad to consume anything that we didn't need. Along with the lawn clippings I dried and stored for their winter fare, these homegrown feeds kept their daily ration of purchased grain at a minimum.

Meat Substitutes and Extenders. These are becoming better known as a result of high meat prices. Much hamburger is now prepared as a mixture of ground beef and a soybean product. Probably most readers have seen and tasted, if they do not regularly use, the "artificial" bacon pieces made from spun soybean protein. There is currently much research on techniques of modifying the texture and flavor of protein foods of plant origin to more closely resemble meat, and this type of product will no doubt prove successful. If a pound of soybean protein equivalent ends up as nearly a pound of protein in a meatlike manufactured product instead of a few ounces as animal flesh, such developments could make significant contributions to our total protein supply.

Improved Leguminous Crops. Soybeans and peanuts have been mentioned as important sources of protein, as are many other members of the legume family, i.e., common beans, lima beans, peas, and a dozen or so other species. They have in common a high protein content in their seeds, but unfortunately crop specialists find it difficult to increase their yields. Soybeans in the United States have been increasing in yield per acre on the average of only one percent per year in recent years while corn was going up at four percent. It is believed by some that the limit of protein yield capacity is reached before the limit of sugar or starch or other carbohydrate. It is true that the crops that produce the greatest tonnages per unit area are relatively low in protein while some high protein crops such as dry edible beans yield only modestly. Much research is under way by plant breeders, soil specialists and crop protection investigators and I am confident they are going to make meaningful progress, but there is no great breakthrough on the horizon comparable to the development of hybrid corn or high yielding dwarf wheats.

Protein Improvement in Grains. Interest in upgrading the genetic capability of plants to produce protein and particularly those amino acid components most likely to be deficient stems from the discovery at Purdue University of a high lysine corn. The mutant gene responsible for this remarkable advance is now being incorporated in varieties with other desirable characters in corn used for human consumption in Latin America and other parts of the world. This development should do much to improve the nutrition of the people who have little access to animal products. Now an intensive search is under way for genetic factors in other food grains and legumes that will give an increased percentage of digestible protein with the right balance of amino acids for superior human nutrition. Several promising leads have been found, and if this work is given adequate support the plant breeders may yet solve many nutritional problems. Poor people in various parts of the world, now dependent on locally raised food, stand little chance of benefiting from advances in animal agriculture or of obtaining improved processed foods. But once supplied with seed of more nutritious varieties they can perpetuate them by saving their own seed and thus benefit year after year.

Chemical Enhancement of Plant Protein

Nitrogen is a primary building block in the plant's synthesis of the amino acids that make up protein molecules. One might therefore assume that increasing the rate of nitrogen fertilization would result in a corresponding increase in protein content. Wide-scale experimentation with grains has shown that only with very high rates of nitrogen fertilization can increased protein percentage be consistently obtained. Economically profitable amounts of fertilizer applied before planting or early in the life of the plant promote more vegetative growth. Higher yields may result, but per unit of potential productivity there is really no increase in the nitrogen available for protein formation at the critical time of seed formation. Recent work indicates that if nitrogen level in the plant can be enhanced during flowering and seed formation, higher protein grain can indeed be obtained. The foliar feeding approach used experimentally may not prove practical for large-scale grain production. Possibly a delayed-release nitrogen fertilizer granule could be devised that would not liberate its nutrients until the time of flowering.

Dr. S. K. Ries and colleagues at Michigan State University have found significant increases in the protein content of various crops when very small doses of certain chemicals are applied to the soil before planting. In some way, these compounds modify protein metabolism, a growth regulator effect that could have far-reaching benefits to mankind. It is too early to predict that higher protein in wheat and other grains will some day be coming from our farms as a result of specialized nitrogen feeding or growth regulator application, but they do offer possibilities for future development. A major part of the protein nourishing the world's four billion people comes from wheat, rice, corn and other cereal grains, and even a one or two percent increase would have tremendous significance. Much research on this subject is yet to be done and it deserves support.

Short-statured grains have made it possible to correct soil mineral deficiencies to get maximum yields without risking the lodging that so often occurs to ordinary tall types if they are well-fertilized and there is wind and heavy rain near harvest time. Note the difference in height between the older type of wheat on the left and a new semi-dwarf variety on the right.

8

Whither the Green Revolution

There is not just one world of nutritional adequacy, diet and food supply. There is the relatively well-fed, technically developed world with land reserves and an efficient agriculture, or lacking these, a reserve of money from other enterprises with which to buy from surplus nations. Here we find western and northern Europe, Canada, Australia and New Zealand, Argentina, Japan, the United States, and a few other isolated countries. Average calorie intake is high and the consumption of meat and other high protein foods far outstrips the world at the other end of the food spectrum.

That is the world where rice, sorghum, millet, maize and cassava provide most of the energy, and relatively little animal protein is available. Hundreds of millions are hungry at least a part of the time, and their protein must come as best it can from plant sources. This world includes India, China, much of the rest of Asia, and tropical Africa.

In between these two extremes is the world where more animal protein is available at least to the affluent, but average intake is modest and grain must provide the bulk of the fuel for the human boiler. Much of Latin America, Russia, eastern Europe, North Africa and the Near East fit this category. The Arab countries with oil to export are now joining the affluent group by importing food.

Averages, of course, can be misleading. Within themselves these worlds have a far from homogeneous diet. There is sometimes dire malnutrition in the midst of plenty even in the United States, and some in the less affluent countries have a luxury diet even where most go hungry. When food is short, prices are high and those with money naturally come out with a better diet. It's easy to decry maldistribution, but the world has never found a way to achieve equitable distribution of a short supply. The first step toward good nutrition for the masses is to be certain there is enough nourishing food to go around.

I promised this would not be a book about food problems in the less developed countries, but to some extent their problems are also ours and an understanding of these different worlds may help us with decisions in the future. Let's look at what is happening in food production in the undernourished parts of the globe.

Progress and Problems

The remarkable increases in yields in the more agriculturally advanced areas, as discussed in chapter 3, did not begin to show up in the less developed countries until the 1960s. The introduction of new, high yielding varieties of wheat, corn and rice specifically for these countries was the key that unlocked the door, while fertilizer and better pest control systems pushed it open a little way. Now it remains to be seen whether these advances which have been termed the Green Revolution will continue. Will the door eventually stand wide open?

The Green Revolution had its origins in the same basic science that brought forth the agricultural revolutions of the past few decades in the more developed countries. Technology transmitted directly from one area to another seldom results in an immediate improvement in productivity. Adaptations are frequently needed to mold it to local conditions. The real spark came with the development in Mexico of some high yielding wheats of dwarf stature and indifference to day length which could be fertilized more heavily and still remain erect in spite of wind and rain. Grain that falls over, or lodges in the language of the agronomist, is difficult to harvest and often suffers severe losses. These wheats were found to be surprisingly well adapted not only to Mexico but also to Pakistan, India and other lower latitude wheat-growing countries where yields were pathetically low. Much credit should be given to the Rockefeller Foundation which supported the International Maize and Wheat Improvement Center in Mexico and made this discovery possible. Credit must also be given to earlier work in wheat genetics in the United States and other countries which served as a scientific foundation for this research. Improved varieties of corn (maize) for lower latitudes also came from this work in Mexico. The importance of improved crop varieties in the eyes of the world was emphasized by the awarding of the Nobel Peace Prize in 1970 to Dr. Norman Borlaug, one of the leading researchers in this international crop improvement program.

This success stimulated further research on improved varieties in a number of places including another foundation-funded regional research center in the Philippines known as the International Rice Research Institute. Here some high yielding rice varieties adapted to South and Southeast Asia were developed. High yields of rice had been obtained for many years in Japan, the United States and some Mediterranean countries, but the varieties used were ill-adapted to heavy fertilization when grown in other climates.

As evidence of the success of the Green Revolution, one has only to look at some comparative yields. Pakistan's 1971 wheat production was up 76 percent from its 1961-65 average, while Latin American corn production was up more than 50 percent and the Indian wheat crop of 1971 was almost double that of six years earlier. Pakistan's 1974 rice crop set an all-time record.

Rice yields increased in the Philippines for a time, however that country has recently had some poor crops because of unfavorable weather. Of course, adverse weather is most often the limiting factor in yields and total productivity, but there is no doubt that improved varieties together with the fertilizer, irrigation and pesticide inputs needed to go along with them have made a significant increase in a number of countries. So far, these achievements have taken place on only a modest part of the land that is devoted to wheat and rice. Now the job is to extend these developments to the food-short parts of the world generally, and also to extend them to crops other than cereals.

There have been many questions raised regarding the true and lasting benefits to be derived from the Green Revolution. Certainly without it several countries would be much shorter of food than they are today, but it is well to take a hard look at some problems that must be overcome.

To a considerable extent, it has been the larger farmers who have benefited. Where production has gone up prices have sometimes come down at harvest time, particularly if the increased yield could not be shipped and stored promptly. Many areas still have woefully inadequate transport and storage facilities. The farmer who obtained greater productivity could still make a profit, but the small farmer without irrigation and whose costs and yields changed little actually had a reduction in income. One of the real challenges is to bring the Green Revolution to the small farmer through better access to credit, small scale irrigation equipment, and the fertilizer and pesticides required to make improved seeds pay off. In many undeveloped regions small farmers control a significant portion of the total agricultural land and unless they too participate in the Green Revolution the potential for total productivity increases is definitely restricted.

The Green Revolution has in some instances reduced the nutritional level of people in farming areas because more emphasis was placed on wheat, rice and corn, and the production of food legumes was lowered. In most low income countries these legumes, which are sometimes called pulses, are widely accepted as dietary staples. Their average consumption is often five times as high as in wealthier countries where more animal protein is available. Increasing cereals at the expense of the edible legumes may only aggravate protein deficiency problems which already exist. Hopefully, productivity of these legumes will eventually increase, but meanwhile those concerned with agronomic development must not concentrate too much on high-carbohydrate cereals and ignore man's need for protein.

Where is the Green Revolution headed? Can the less developed countries possibly expand their food production at a greater rate than population? And if they can do so during the next few years how long can they sustain this agricultural growth? By increasing productivity now, are they merely postponing the day when the need for food will so outdistance supply that massive famine will result? Will they ever arrive at a point where they can have good reserves to take care of a lean year or will they always have to look abroad for food to make up a deficiency?

In answering these questions, it may be well to refer back to the things needed to keep our supermarket shelves filled as discussed in chapter 2. It is true that less developed countries may have a different distribution system and there is often much more reliance on locally produced food. Even so, the same factors are needed to increase productivity on a sustained basis. Farmers must have an incentive and they must have the land and the water either from rain or irrigation. They can't produce big yields without good varieties, but they must also have the fertilizer needed to nourish them and the chemicals needed to protect them from insects and diseases. The infrastructure must be there to encourage and support agricultural production. Without storage and transportation, market gluts and resulting low prices are inevitable. Whether one is operating within a free enterprise system or a centrally planned economy, credit has to be available in some form. Just having an improved and potentially high yielding variety alone will do little good. All these other factors have to fit in place.

I believe there will continue to be improvements in the production of cereals in many less developed countries, and the great effort now being expended to extend the Green Revolution to other food crops to make a better rounded diet will pay off. But every country has to work at it. Their leaders must give high priority to support for agricultural projects. Food production and storage projects have often been starved of local financing because leaders saw reserves in the developed countries as a bottomless grain bin to which they could turn at the first sign of hunger. Now that they know the bin is empty, perhaps they will begin to give their own farmers and technologists the support they must have if their often underutilized capacity is to be realized.

In addition to agricultural research funded by local governments, several foundations are now pooling their resources to support regional efforts in Asia, Latin America and Africa. There is much current research aimed at improved nutritional properties in crops adapted to the less developed countries. Significant effort is being put forth to increase the production of fish in ponds and, in many instances, develop dairy, poultry, and livestock enterprises. These should contribute to a better diet and, if not too dependent on the importation of feed, they should also be of value to the economy.

Unfortunately, much of the world has only begun to utilize the commodity protection technology that has already been developed and is in common use in the more advanced countries. It has been estimated by authorities on the scene that 15 percent of all the rice and other cereal crops raised in the Orient are destroyed by rats, either in the field or in storage. Fifteen percent of Asia's cereal crops must be equated with nearly 50 million acres, an area the size of the entire State of Kansas. Losses to rodents are appreciable everywhere, but integrated control programs, including the use of chemical rodenticides as one important phase, are reasonably successful where they are undertaken on a sustained basis. Insects too take a terrific toll of stored grain and other products in less developed countries.

In our more technically advanced world, modern fumigation and other control methods have so reduced the infestation of dry food products that few housewives reading this can conceive of the losses still suffered by their counterparts in, say, India or central Africa. How long since you have thrown out wormy flour? The housewife in India might not discard such flour but she is well acquainted with infesting worms and bugs.

The Green Revolution will not be meaningful to people of the poorly fed parts of the world unless it is accompanied by construction of storage facilities properly managed for rodent and insect control. Increased yields mean only gluts and ruinous prices at harvest time with staggering losses unless the infrastructure needed to protect, transport and distribute the food is in existence or is developed parallel to improved crop production methods. Storage losses anywhere are equated with more acres planted to satisfy human needs and less space remaining to contribute to the recreational and other nonagricultural uses of land so essential to the kind of environment we hope to achieve.

Relationships of the Different Worlds

If you are confused about what you read concerning the present food situation in the less developed countries and their prospects for the future, you have a lot of company. Glowing press reports of progress with the Green Revolution one day are often followed by a news item about impending famine the next. What is the true picture? What can we expect during the next decade and beyond? I believe there will continue to be a widely swinging pendulum. Progress is being made in improving food production in most parts of the world but few countries have reserves to provide for lean years. So when there is a drought or flood there will have to be belt tightening and there will no doubt sometimes be dire malnutrition and actual famine as is currently (early 1975) being reported from India and Bangladesh. By our standards, there is much hunger throughout the less developed world as there almost always has been in the past.

Just where hunger ends and famine begins is hard to say. It is not that people fail to recognize the value of a food grain reserve. Their hand-to-mouth existence has largely been forced on them through circumstances including relentless population increase.

Not so many years ago a number of the currently food-short countries were exporters of grain as well as other commodities. Then population caught up with slowly increasing agricultural productivity. In recent years the United States and Canada have been the chief exporters of cereals for food and feeds. Now expanded population, a luxury diet at home and a marked increase in cash customers have erased the surpluses that once could be drawn upon for relief of hungry nations. What will happen if there is a prolonged drought in a country presently on the rocky edge? India, Bangladesh, and China are especially vulnerable because they feed so little livestock and there is thus little grain to be diverted to human use. Don't be surprised if the greatest famine in history occurs somewhere in the next decade. After all, there are a lot more people to be hungry than in the past and the danger spots are growing in population at two percent and upward each year.

Given a decent break in the weather (which seldom happens on a sustained basis) and new technology, the Green Revolution should enable most parts of the world to show food production improvements adequate to keep their people alive and possibly even feed them a little better for a few years. But then there is that "Population Bomb" ever-ready to explode. There are many social, economic and environmental reasons for controlling population but all of these would fade into oblivion if there was not enough food to go around. The figures I have seen on continuing high birthrates in most of the less developed countries do not indicate very rapid progress in birth control. Unless there is a revolution in family size, it is very doubtful that food production increases can continue to keep pace for long, even given good growing conditions. The population of many countries will double in little more than a generation at present growth rates.

The most startling arithmetic or population growth was pointed out by Nathan Keyfitz in a recent issue of *Demography.* He calculated that if by some miracle a typical less developed country could lower its birthrate to the replacement level by the year 2000 it would nonetheless reach two and one-half times its present size before it stopped growing. There must be a demographic revolution in these countries. If they take as long as we have in industrialized countries to significantly cut their birthrates, there is little hope of avoiding famines.

What should be the policy of the more technically advanced countries with their declining birthrates and their safety valve in the form of huge quantities of grain now fed to livestock? Hopefully we can again build reserves that would permit at least selective aid when needed by those countries that are progressing with both birth control and an improved agricultural technology. Possibly some kind of an international food reserve is desirable. However, I cannot help but agree with the Paddock brothers in their book, *Famine 1975,* that in time of extreme hunger the policy of shipping reserves to those who have shown little ability to control their population or significantly increase food production has little to recommend it. Would we not just be keeping more people alive to be even hungrier again when the next shortage occurs; hungrier and perhaps starving along with the additional multitudes added to the population each year.

This is not a pleasant subject to think or write about, but there is nothing to be gained by brushing the population-food facts of life under the rug. We have an infinite capacity to reproduce but a very finite capacity to increase food production. Speaking of the world as a whole, in the past, new land and new technology has kept food supply in pace with population, with a few deficiencies here and surpluses there. Now the new land is about used up and we are depending on improved technology. This can sustain us for a while but the potential for technical improvements is finite too. There can be no light at the end of the tunnel unless population is brought under control.

The future success of the Green Revolution and the success of the less developed countries in bringing their population growth in check will have a tremendous impact on you. In recent years, the food surplus countries really have no surplus to speak of. Grain supplies in the world are at the lowest level in decades, and probably the lowest in a century on a per capita basis. We are certain to have more requests for help from food-short countries. What should be done?

More and more questions like this will come up, and the tighter the food situation is in the less developed countries the more pleas we will hear when a flood or drought causes supply to drop below minimum needs. It is not going to be pleasant to live in a world with so many poor people short of food. Perhaps this is looking at it selfishly, but I think we have much to gain if we can help extend the Green Revolution and contribute to population control just because we will have fewer requests for aid. It is not going to make life in the developed countries any more pleasant if we do not supply relief where genuinely needed. So perhaps in the interest of peace of mind for the future, if not for present humanitarian reasons, we should extend ourselves to promote more efficient food production abroad and the population control that is necessary if increased food is to have a lasting benefit.

The decision for surplus countries to sell food is easy if there are big reserves, but what if our grain storages are far from bulging or not even carrying a modest reserve as a prudent safeguard against the prospect of lean years at home? Should each agricultural country have an "ever-normal granary" and use only an excess beyond a minimum reserve for trade and aid? This is a tough question, but let's think about it now. Some day it will have to be answered. Export restrictions have already had to be instituted in some instances. I am hopeful that favorable weather and all that goes to insure bountiful harvests will make the day of further restrictions in trade far off. But with a continuing rapid increase in population in most parts of the world and the ever-present chance of a yield-depressing drought, such as experienced in the "breadbasket" of North America in the 1930's, that day might not be so far off.

Certainly the rapidly growing and agriculturally less developed countries face monumental problems and there is perhaps not a lot we can do for them. But one thing is certain. Any improvements in productivity they achieve are most likely to stem from adaptations of science and technology transmitted from our world, the world of bountiful harvests and full market shelves. As you enjoy your next meal, determine to support those programs that can enable us to learn more about making optimum use of our agricultural resources. If we can keep our yield revolution and our soil-building revolution going, it will certainly benefit us, and some benefits are likely to spill over to less fortunate people.

Only in greenhouses has it proven practical to increase crop productivity by supplementing the normal carbon dioxide of the atmosphere, but much research is in progress on possible field approaches to enriching this building block of photosynthesis. Here the effect of increasing carbon dioxide on soybean yields is being studied under field conditions. This research showed that improved photosynthesis results in greater nitrogen fixation and significantly increased yields of this important crop.

9

New Technology on The Horizon

"And he gave it as his opinion, that whoever could make two ears of corn or two blades of grass grow upon a spot of ground where only one grew before, would deserve better of mankind, and do more essential service to his country, than the whole race of politicians put together."

Jonathan Swift
in Gulliver's Travels

My interest in improved agricultural technology started with Paul DeKruif's book, *Hunger Fighters,* which was on a reading list for ninth grade English. His story of the early breeders who gave us rust-resistant wheat and other plant improvements convinced me that I, too, wanted to help advance food production technology. During my forty years in agricultural research and development with a seed company, two universities and an agricultural chemical manufacturer, I have watched with fascination the introduction and subsequent commercialization of a host of technical advances.

As an agronomy student at the University of Minnesota, I helped harvest hybrid corn yield plots in some of the early trials, and it was thrilling to see the 25 percent greater

yield we often obtained over the farmers' best strains. It
was like being in the crew of a ship charting a shoreline never
seen before. I was only an observer, although a fascinated
one, of the early use of anhydrous ammonia as a cheap source
of nitrogen for crop nutrition, an agricultural development
I would rate along with hybrid corn as among the more important of all time. Another candidate for top honors where
I have had the good fortune to be a participant, is the discovery and development of selective herbicides, astonishing chemicals that kill or stunt damaging weeds without hurting
the crop.

While on the faculty of Michigan State University in a co-
operative project with Dr. Thomas W. Whitaker of the U.S.
Department of Agriculture, I had the privilege of first identify-
ing a more vigorous heat-resistant strain of head lettuce which
we named Great Lakes. For many years it has been the leading
variety in major lettuce growing regions and through higher
average yields has helped keep salad on your table. I've followed
the research of professional friends and colleagues who sparked
many facets of the poultry revolution which has given us chicken
and turkey, once luxuries, at a cost below most other meats.
Here was an astonishing improvement in production efficiency
based on breeding, better nutrition, and improved disease control, all combined with new management practices. Poultry
would still be a luxury for special occasions if any one of those
had been left out.

So much for reminiscences. This is not to be a catalog
of past research accomplishments but rather a peek at the
future. Having seen so many developments that gave us today's
productive agriculture, I naturally have a high level of interest in new science and technology on the horizon that may
help keep market shelves well-stocked indefinitely. Some
have already been mentioned. Here are highlights of additional new discoveries that I think you will hear more about.
There are many others of course. Consider this only as a
sampler.

Plant Growth Regulators

These are not new. You may have used a regulator spray to im-prove the early set of tomatoes or perhaps a powder in which to dip the stems of cuttings to hasten rooting. The 2, 4-D or silvex you have used to selectively remove dandelions and other broad leaf weeds from your lawn are really growth regulators. Used in adequate doses, they cause some kinds of plants to grow abnormally and die. But there are new dimensions in growth regulators on the horizon; new uses not just to alter morphology or growth patterns but to change chemical com-position, modify metabolism and increase yield. Improved latex flow in rubber trees and increased sugar content of cane stalks are examples being commercialized or ready to use as soon as human and environmental safety checks are completed. One of my colleagues has experimentally increased protein in a root crop and improved oil percentage in soybeans. Some researchers have reported an increase in the protein content of grain follow-ing the application of a minute amount of a common herbicide.

Research workers at a number of commercial laboratories and publicly funded institutions are delving into the biochemical mysteries of plant respiration and I will not be surprised if growth regulators are found that will control it. Green plants using light as a source of energy carry on photosynthesis to build carbohydrates from carbon dioxide and water. Oxygen is left over as a by-product. Respiration is the reverse chemical reac-tion. Carbohydrates are oxidized to give off carbon dioxide and water. Obviously, in order to grow, plants must carry on photo-synthesis faster than they do respiration or there would be no net gain. Recently plant physiologists have found that our high-est yielding crops, corn for example, carry on less respiration particularly during daylight hours than some other crops, such as wheat. Is this why we have never been able to make wheat yield as much as corn? I'll gamble that plant scientists will learn how to slow down respiration either by genetic or chemical means and thereby achieve a greater net gain from photosynthesis.

More efficient photosynthesis will not result in higher yields of grain, storage tubers or roots unless sugars are transported efficiently within the plant. There is some evidence that chemical growth regulators may improve translocation and thus increase yield of storage organs. Both the growth regulator people and the breeder are working toward plants that have a different geometry so that leaves are better oriented to the sun so as to trap more of its energy. They have already made much progress toward stronger stemmed plants, ones that can be given the optimum nutrition needed for high yields without risk of lodging.

Carbon Dioxide Supplementation

Think of a crop plant as a factory. The end product is the grain or fruit or other plant part that you eat or that is fed to livestock or poultry. Raw materials and energy are needed just as they are in any factory. The plant gets its energy from the sun in the form of light to make the manufacturing process (photosynthesis) go and in the form of solar heat to keep the factory space warm. No meaningful plant growth takes place at too low a temperature even though light and raw material supply is adequate.

The raw materials that must go into the hopper of this factory are (1) carbon dioxide from the air surrounding the plant and (2) water, mostly from the soil. Also needed are (3) mineral nutrients largely brought into the plant with this water. Good farmers and gardeners now supply the minerals they need and many can supply water. But only a modest part of our total cropping area receives irrigation, so when rainfall is short water becomes the limiting factor in productivity.

Carbon dioxide (CO_2) has long been recognized as an essential building block for plant growth but only in recent years has it been clear that the 300 parts per million normally in the atmosphere is not enough for a maximum rate of growth if other factors are favorable. Thus CO_2 often becomes the limiting factor in crop productivity. CO_2, like other gasses, is elusive stuff since it diffuses rapidly. Only greenhouse growers of vegetables and ornamentals have found it practical to increase the CO_2 content of the atmosphere surrounding their plants and thereby increase yields, but many scientists are working on systems for high value field-grown crops. Tremendous amounts of CO_2 pass out of every chimney and much is available from geologic sources. If we can find some way to get it to the crop and keep it there until it diffuses into the cells where photosynthesis goes on, plant growth rates could be materially increased.

Making Water Go Further

No one with a lawn or garden needs to be reminded that water is the most frequent limiting factor in plant growth. Prodigious amounts pass up through growing plants and are lost as vapor through the stomata, those tiny openings in the leaf that open and close with diurnal changes and varying environmental conditions. This process of vapor loss is known as transpiration. Much water vapor is also lost by evaporation from the soil surface. Mulching with organic materials or plastic film and close plant spacing to shade the ground reduce this loss.

Although the major function of stomata is to permit passage of carbon dioxide and oxygen into and out of the leaf, they have a profound effect on the amount of water required for plant growth. Now chemicals that modify the opening and closing habits of stomata have been found and research indicates that partial closing of these leaf openings will reduce water vapor loss without inhibiting growth. Apparently gas exchange can still take place between the atmosphere and the interior of the leaf.

While plant physiologists have been making progress in regulating stomatal closing as an approach to raising crops with less water, the engineers have made an important contribution with the development of trickle irrigation. This type of water application had been used for some time in greenhouses and with very high-value plants in the field, but only now does it appear practical for major crops.

In trickle irrigation (sometimes called drip irrigation), plastic tubing laid along the row drips water at so slow a pace that there is no problem of soil washing even on rolling land. The trickle of water enters the soil without wetting the entire surface, thus reducing evaporation greatly. Experience in Israel, Hawaii and California indicates that the water available for irrigation will provide for increased crop acreage when this system can be used and yields will often be increased as a result of more uniform soil moisture conditions. Drip irrigation is not adapted to soils that are high in soluble salts since these require copious amounts of water and good drainage so the excess salts will be kept below the zone of root growth.

Targeting Pesticides

When 2,4-D was still in the experimental stages of development back in 1945, some exploratory work I saw at the New York Experiment Station at Geneva indicated the material would translocate downward from a cut made in the bark of a woody plant. At the time I was engaged in research on the control of undesirable woody plants such as those growing in pastures, and this finding prompted further tests which I conducted on several species. Cut stumps, or frills in bark and also undisturbed bark were treated with oil solutions of 2,4-D and related compounds. From this came methods now in wide use for targeting herbicide applications. Using basal bark or frill applications, many millions of acres of potentially good grazing land have been converted to grass by killing the competing worthless woody plants. In Australia, particularly, a significant increase in pasture-carrying capacity has been achieved by these systems of weed-tree and brush control.

Having participated in this one phase of target hitting with pesticides, I have been following with considerable interest the more recent research on making a given amount of chemical more efficient. There is already a lessening tendency for farmers to apply weed, insect and disease control chemicals blindly without the best equipment or the most desirable formulation. Pesticide targeting involves both proper timing, minimum effective doses, and the most efficient method of application. Expanded knowledge on the part of the applicator is insuring the best timing so the desired effect is obtained with as few applications as possible, and, meanwhile, better engineering has given us vastly improved application equipment.

Good growers no longer spray at the appearance of the first damaging bug but check populations and apply at the time experimentation has shown is best for the greatest economic return. In the future the new insect attractants, or pheromones as they are called, will no doubt be useful for more accurately determining populations, and through this the need for and the timing of application for optimum results. The control of spray droplet size is increasing insecticide efficiency and thereby lowering costs and minimizing chances of an adverse environmental effect. In the area of animal insect control, the flea collar your dog wears is not the only highly targeted approach. Cattle now receive their annual systemic grub control treatment through a dipperful of solution poured on the animal's back rather than a drenching spray.

In the herbicide area, drift control additives are becoming very important while directed sprays in crops are minimizing dosage and optimizing weed control. Some herbicides are incorporated into the soil before planting and some are even placed in a zone below the soil surface where the lowest dosage will have the greatest effect. Remote sensing from space vehicles can help determine the onset of disease in crops and thus aid growers in deciding just when a fungicide application is needed. New technology related to targeting of pesticides is just as important as having the right compound not only from the standpoint of efficacy and environmental safety but also from the economic point of view. Much progress is being made in integrated insect management designed to utilize natural control mechanisms together with resistant varieties and insecticides as needed to reduce damaging peak populations.   Insecticide targeting is an essential part of such programs.

Improved Nitrogen Nutrition of Plants

Crops need nitrogen as a building block for protein from the time growth begins, and, to be highly productive, their requirements go up as their size increases.   The amount of nitrogen required for the final stages of vegetative development is many times the amount needed for early growth.   The problem is that nitrogen fertilizer applied in adequate amounts before planting may leach below the zone of root growth if there is heavy rain. Split applications, with a part of the fertilizer going on before planting and a part after the crop is started, is a traditional way, often successful, of insuring nitrogen for that final spurt of growth that is needed for top yields.

You may have used urea-formaldehyde resin, a slow-release fertilizer on your lawn.   Other special slow-release fertilizers are used for potted plants and nursery stock.   These have not been economical for wide scale use but now two new approaches are showing great promise.   First is a granular nitrogen fertilizer coated with sulfur.   This is essentially a slow-release form that will be partially available for early growth, but the rest is more likely to be there in the right amount to push the plant over the finish line.

The other is a chemical, applied with the fertilizer, that inhibits the growth of the bacteria that convert the ammonia form of nitrogen to nitrate.   Ammonia does not leach since the molecules hang on to soil colloids and percolating rain water does not move them below the root zone.   But the existence of nitrogen fertilizer in the ammonia form is transitory since these nitrifying bacteria soon convert the ammonia to nitrate, a form readily taken up by the plant but also readily moved downward if heavy rain occurs.   By inhibiting the growth of these bacteria in the zone of soil where the fertilizer is placed, the ammonia is stabilized and the chances of leaching greatly reduced.   Major farm crops can take up their needed nitrogen either as ammonia or as nitrate so the use of a nitrification inhibitor to slow down conversion to the latter will reduce the chances of pollution of ground water or streams and at the same time insure better crop nutrition. The inhibitor-treated fertilizer is usually banded in the soil so that only cylinders of soil at intervals receive the inhibitor. After it has degraded, normal soil flora invade the zone. I believe the future will see wide use of nitrification inhibitors applied in mixture with ammonia fertilizers as a means of protecting the environment and maximizing yields.

The ability of certain kinds of bacteria to fix atmospheric nitrogen when growing in root nodules in symbiotic union with clover, beans and other legumes has long been recognized. We have taken advantage of this phenomenon by modifying soil conditions to favor both legumes and the bacteria, for example, by liming and applying phosphate and potash. Free-living forms of microorganisms that fix nitrogen have been discovered but no practical way has been found to cause them to increase to the point that they would substitute for nitrogen fertilizer. They do, however, make a significant contribution to the soil's nitrogen supply, particularly in flooded rice land.

Recently a Brazilian researcher has found that another type of bacteria which grows in association with certain tropical grasses can fix nitrogen in adequate amounts to nourish the host plant. If similar bacteria could be found that would grow on the roots of corn, wheat and other major cereal crops, we could not only insure better yields but also save the tremendous amount of natural gas now required for the world's nitrogen fertilizer production. The petroleum crisis has stimulated much research aimed at this target.

Systemic Fungicides

A century has elapsed since it was discovered that a concoction containing copper sulfate would control grape mildew. According to legend, a farmer near Bordeau, France, in exasperation, sprayed some prized vines to discourage boys of the neighborhood from stealing his grapes. Wherever the blue residue had wet the leaves mildew did not develop. We do not know how discouraging the treatment was to the boys but the discovery had profound benefit for all of us. For many decades Bordeau Mixture, as a formulation of copper sulfate and lime came to be called, was the fungicide treatment that eliminated potato blight as a threat to our food supply. With this fungus control material available, another Irish potato famine could not occur. Sigotoka of bananas and several other diseases of fruits and vegetables that were often catastrophic were kept in check with this mixture.

A number of improved fungicides whose activity is based on a particular molecular configuration rather than the copper ion were discovered in the 1930s and later, but until very recently most of them required rather complete leaf coverage. Fungus spores landing on the leaves germinated and then were killed or inhibited in growth because of the fungitoxic nature of the compound covering the plant. Recently new breakthroughs have occurred in several commercial research laboratories devoted to improved agricultural chemicals in the form of systemic fungicides. No longer is success dependent on very complete coverage and no longer does one have to respray after every rain. The toxicant is absorbed and can move internally at least to the extent that the entire leaf is protected, even though only a portion of it was covered with the spray. We appear to be on the threshold of valuable new developments in the systemic control of a range of plant diseases.

Asexual Aids to Plant Improvement

Just as you marvel at the beauty of a new rose or lily, the crop specialist gets a thrill out of a new variety or hybrid resistant to a disease or in some other way capable of improved productivity. Most early plant breeding merely involved selection of chance variations. Then hybridization to increase variability came into practice. More recently emphasis has been on the commercialization of hybrid vigor by using large scale cross pollination techniques for seed production. None of these methods have lost their importance but now there are new horizons for the plant breeder in the form of asexual aids to crop improvement.

It started with basic studies by botanists interested in plant cell development. They found that individual vegetative cells of some plants could be isolated and then made to develop into a complete new plant by growing on a special nutrient medium. Thus a new form of vegetative propagation became available, one which could speed up the increase of desirable specimen plants arising from hybridization.

Orchid breeders were the first to use the technique variously called meristeming, cell culture, tissue culture or micropropagation. Instead of being satisfied with the dozen or so offspring of a new hybrid normally obtainable by division, they could now produce thousands. Now this method is being evaluated with many kinds of plants.

A number of vegetatively propagated crops can be infected with viruses. Cell culture is a method of obtaining virus-free stock of such species as sugar cane, potatoes, and raspberries. The genetic makeup of a desirable variety is maintained but the virus which would pass on to the vegetative progeny if conventional bulbs, tubers, cuttings or root divisions were resorted to can be eliminated with cell culture techniques.

The more recent and exciting aspect of tissue culture as an aid to plant improvement relates to the fusion of protoplasts of vegetative cells of different plants, thus forming hybrids without going through the often difficult process of cross pollination. I am hopeful that many interspecific and even intergeneric hybrids can be formed in this way. Our new ability to raise plants from single cells may also make it possible to propagate induced somatic mutations resulting from gene or chromosome modifications. Some imaginative experiments are now underway using pollen cultures for producing haploid plants, a short cut to the time-consuming inbreeding normally required for obtaining "pure" or homozygous lines. We've seen some marvelous plant improvements in the past but the art and science of plant breeding may be only in its infancy.

Cattle Nutrition

Some basic aspects of nutrition of cattle and other ruminants as compared with poultry and swine were discussed in chapter 7. You will recall everything a cow eats is digested in its fermentation vat called the rumen. A bovine animal or a sheep doesn't have to be fed a proper balance of amino acids as long as enough fixed nitrogen to nourish the bacteria gets into the mix. Ordinarily all this nitrogen would come from protein but in recent years it has been learned that cattle can derive a part of their nitrogen requirements, or one should really say the bacteria in the rumen can derive theirs, from cheaper nonprotein sources. Feedstuffs are sometimes treated with ammonia but, more commonly, urea is used in the rations of feedlot cattle to supply as much as one-half the animal's nitrogen requirements. This saves money for the feedlot operator and conserves protein for other uses.

But only the final part of the beef animal's life is spent in a feedlot. While on pasture or range the animal may get plenty of energy from grass, but unless it is of especially good quality there will not be enough protein in it to provide the bacteria in the rumen with all they need. As the animal's growth is dependent on bacterial protein digested in its alimentary system beyond the rumen, grass must often be supplemented with a nitrogen source for optimum weight gains. Ranchers once gave animals seedmeal cake but this source of nitrogen is now very expensive. Urea cannot be used safely for supplying very much of the nitrogen needs of cattle on range or pasture. They would tend to ingest too much of it at once when they visited a feeding trough. Ammonia is generated rather quickly when urea enters the rumen, and too much ammonia over a short period is hard on both the animal and the rumen organisms.

A search for alternate forms of nonprotein nitrogen has revealed some that are promising for low-cost supplementation of animals on range and pasture. Biuret is one that appears safe for them to consume at will at a feeding station which they may visit only once a day. Ammonia is liberated gradually from biuret like a slow-release fertilizer for your lawn. With the current high cost of grain and our present knowledge of ways to improve pastures and range, it will become increasingly important to have nonprotein nitrogen supplements like biuret. As such supplements become more widely available, the length of time animals are kept on grass can increase with correspondingly lower costs.

Nutritionists are not satisfied with nonprotein nitrogen sources as the only way to economize in cattle feeding operations. Some visualized the possibility of finding a way to cause proteins to pass through the rumen without being torn apart by bacteria and thus give the animal an enriched protein diet, hopefully resulting in more rapid growth. This was merely a wild-eyed dream until not long ago when investigations in Australia and elsewhere indicated that, by certain methods of processing, protein can be protected from bacterial attack in the rumen and yet be available to the animal when it reaches the rest of its digestive tract. There is a lot of research and engineering to complete before commercialization, but it does appear likely that cattle feeding can become more efficient using such a scheme. The rumen will still function and need nitrogen to support bacterial growth, but additional protein passing through it in a protected form should improve rates of gain and someday contribute to a better supply of beef and lamb at your local market, and help make wool more abundant. This new technology could also have a significant impact on the efficiency of milk production.

Improving Reproductive Efficiency

If a cow was as efficient as a hen reproductively she would have between two and three hundred calves each year. Preposterous, of course, but she should be able to do better than the less than one offspring per year now averaged in cattle operations. A brood sow doesn't hold a candle to the hen but the two dozen or more piglets she raises a year put her way ahead of the cow. Improvements in nutrition and disease control and breeding for more rapid gains are all important, but the real breakthrough in cattle raising would come if reproductive efficiency could be significantly improved. Remember that the cost of maintenance of a mother animal must be spread over her offspring. If a mother cow now averaging less than one per year could produce two, the change would have a significant effect on the price of beef at your supermarket. We have produced two ears of corn and two blades of grass where there used to be one. Can we make it two calves?

It is too early to make predictions but current extensive studies on the physiology of reproduction may someday give us young animals for growing on to slaughter size at a significantly lower cost. Controlled induction of twinning in cattle and sheep and more than one lamb crop per year are possibilities being investigated. The modification of animal sex ratios is also under investigation and holds some promise for the future. The control of the period of estrus in a group of animals to permit batch farrowing is another aspect of reproduction control that could have economic benefit and is a definite possibility through the use of ovulatory regulators. Embryo implantation techniques now being practiced by animal breeders will make it possible to speed up reproduction of superior mother cows just as artificial insemination has aided in passing on the outstanding genetic inheritance of selected male animals to a large number of offspring. There is no way these advances in the physiology of reproduction can make meat cheap since it is inevitably a luxury. But they would contribute to keeping costs within a range that we can afford.

Research and development related to your future food supply goes on. Some is successful and much fails. It often takes as much hard work and brainpower to find out what won't work as what will. There has recently been much criticism of publicly supported agricultural research. Some of this is deserving but much stems from the fact that many research people, particularly those highly trained and devoted to fundamental studies, tend to look down on the grubby job of putting their findings to work. All will agree that it was some outstanding research in plant physiology going all the way back to Charles Darwin that led to synthetic growth regulators as practical tools for improving crop productivity. But how about the final and important step of determining precise dosage and timing of application and effects on quality? How about the field studies on yield increases needed to define the economic value of a growth regulator application? Perhaps the hangup comes when this important technical work is called research. Perhaps it should be referred to as development or just technology. But no matter what it is called it is important and has to be done.

More food, better food and cheaper food will not reach your market shelves from basic research alone. Even when this is followed by what we often call applied research there will be no public benefit until all the technical details are worked out and the method or the product made available to the farmer. Neither will future technical progress be possible unless we maintain a high level of basic research on a wide front. New and useful food production technology stems from a long sequence beginning with basic studies often unrelated to agriculture, through more applied research though still of a fundamental nature, on to application investigations and finally to a myriad of developmental details. It all deserves your continuing support.

Farm ponds, now dot the landscape of rolling and hilly land, particularly in the southeastern United States. In addition to providing water for livestock and irrigation, ponds hold back flood waters following heavy rain. They further improve the environment by supporting fish and encouraging other forms of wildlife.

10

Energy and Your Food Supply

Since the oil crisis of late 1973 little is spoken or written about our future without at least a passing comment on energy problems. Plans and actions aimed at insuring a continuing abundance of food require more than passing recognition that petroleum and electricity are vital to the food of your future if our present system of production, processing, and distribution is to continue. If food is our number one need, then the energy required to produce it and put it on your supermarket shelf must be at the very top of any priority list.

I recently heard a TV commentator, adding his bit to the oil controversy, say that our farms and forests use solar energy, that plants grow through the benefit of the sun's rays. He left it there without adding that with our modern system of production and distribution and our luxury diets the fossil fuel energy we indirectly use to feed ourselves often equals or exceeds that which crop plants capture from the sun.

Dr. George Borgstrom has pointed out how much of our food today is made possible only because long ago nature stored the sun's energy in the form of fossil fuels. His calculations indicate that in countries consuming large amounts of livestock products we actually expend more energy in production than we obtain back as food. We are eating up our fossil fuel bank account just as we are expending it on heat, transportation and manufactured goods.

Think again about your breakfast! The sun provided the energy needed to support growth of a coffee bush in Brazil, an orange tree in Florida, a wheat field in North Dakota. But the sun didn't roast the coffee, concentrate and freeze the juice or convert the wheat to bread. If you had bacon and eggs, the energy needed to run the tractors and supply the fertilizer for corn and soybean fields figured high in your daily withdrawal from our petroleum bank account. And the sun didn't transport your coffee all the way from Brazil or provide the glass jar it came in. It didn't run your refrigerator or heat your stove. The sun only runs the photosynthesis machine. We have to do the rest, and it takes a lot of doing.

Early man had only his own muscle to supplement the sun. Then for thousands of years he used beasts of burden for tillage and transportation. The wind drove ships and turned mills for pumping water and grinding grain. Flowing water also converted grain to flour. Then gradually with the advent of the industrial revolution we began to be more dependent on machines which directly or indirectly used fossil fuels as their source of power. To a considerable extent these fuels have made possible our tremendous increase in total food production, a growth that has, except in a few times and places, kept pace with a rapidly expanding population. Let's look a little further at our dependence on energy for our food supply, on what it means for the future and particularly how we may continue to have abundance with less extravagant use of energy than we have known in recent years.

A tough food question we almost certainly will have to answer in the future is the one of allocation of energy resources to the farm. I doubt that we will stand for crops rotting in the field because tractor fuel is unavailable while cars whiz by often transporting only the driver. What good will a vacation trip do us if the bread truck and milk truck and the big semis that deliver food from the warehouse can't get supplies to where we are? Allocation or rationing of petroleum is not a pleasant thought but we may some day need it if we are to avoid food rationing and continue to have well-stocked shelves at the supermarket. Petroleum reserves are finite and sooner or later, probably within the lifetime of you younger readers, priorities on its use will have to be established.

Next to motor fuel for operating farm equipment and energy for food processing and distribution, fertilizer is the most energy-demanding facet of your daily food supply. Currently most nitrogen fertilizer is produced from hydrogen derived from natural gas. Other fertilizer components which are mined or pumped from wells require much energy for processing and distribution. A few hungry days or an occasional empty shelf at the supermarket would quickly convince us that if energy must some day be rationed, fertilizer production and shipment should be kept high on the priority list. I am hopeful that more nitrogen can be fixed in the soil through the wider use of legumes and possibly through the encouragement of nitrogen fixing organisms not now widely distributed. But even with optimism regarding such developments much energy will still be needed to make and ship the fertilizer essential to good yields.

Energy for fertilizer and motor fuel is not all that may some day have to be allocated if food shortages are to be avoided. In the wet fall of 1972, grain dryers in the central United States were unable to operate at times because of a shortage of propane gas. We came close to having significant spoilage. Perhaps farmers should turn back to harvesting ear corn and storing it in slat or wire cribs for gradual drying as was always practical until recent years. This is one way we can utilize solar energy just as a housewife could again use it for drying clothes.

Most methods of crop processing require an energy source in the form of electricity, gas, petroleum or coal. Not long ago there was a threat of a fuel shortage at a sugar plant in Michigan that would have prevented the beets in storage from being processed. My home may be warm next winter, but I could not really be comfortable if huge piles of sugar beets were going to waste.

There is no way to get food in usable form from the farm to your kitchen without containers. True, we have become accustomed to many disposable types. Simpler containers and more returnable ones could and I think should be used, but no matter how you look at it, considerable energy for food container manufacture will always be essential. I hope we do not have to go back to the days when milk arrived at your door in bulk and was ladled into the purchaser's tin bucket.

Electricity is used in very large volumes to get food to your kitchen. Think of the electric energy required by milking machines, cold storage plants and the frozen food display cabinets at your market, not to mention the operation of tens of thousands of irrigation pumps.

Upward of 200 million tons of corn, sorghum, soybeans, wheat and barley are produced each year in the heartland of North America, that great grain country that stretches from Texas on the south to the Peace River country far north in Canada. Harvest begins in June and is wrapped up in the fall. At very best it is a strain to get this stupendous quantity to ports for shipment abroad and to storages in many locations at home for conversion to flour, cooking oil and feedstuffs. Railroads have been the backbone of the transportation system that moves it. Far less energy per ton mile is required to move these heavy bulk items by rail than other methods of land transport. We should think twice about the next generation's energy supply and food needs before we let the railroads serving grain growing regions be abandoned or fall into disrepair.

If you drive into a gasoline station in Brazil and say "fill it up", chances are the liquid the attendant pumps into your tank will consist of 85 percent gasoline and 15 percent alcohol, the latter produced by the fermentation of molasses, a by-product of the huge cane sugar industry in that country. Thus Brazilian cane farmers are helping keep their country on the move. Alcohol can be produced from any fermentable plant material so why can't agriculture make its own motor fuel for tractors or trucks? Technically speaking it can, but until the 1973 jump in petroleum prices the economics of making alcohol for its energy value was generally unfavorable. Brazil had a special situation. The one pound of molasses obtained as a by-product with each four pounds of sugar produced in her many sugar factories costs too much to ship abroad for cattle feed or other uses and it makes economic sense to convert it to motor fuel for domestic use, particularly because so much petroleum had to be imported. Now with our new petroleum economics, alcohol or blends of it with gasoline could come closer to competing elsewhere for use in motor vehicles, but land now used for food crops must be reserved to fuel the human machine. Possibly other fermentable agricultural by-products can be used for limited production of alcohol for motor fuel.

The old but little used technology of acid hydrolysis of the cellulose in wood to sugars followed by fermentation to alcohol may appear more economically sound in the future. Recent research suggests that the long-dreamed-of efficient enzymatic method of converting cellulose from trees and agricultural wastes to sugars may yet be realized. Waste paper may also be converted to fermentable sugars. After all, the plant made the sugars first through photosynthesis and then used sugar molecules as building blocks to form cellulose, the major component of plant fiber. I think man will eventually prove smart enough to discover an efficient way to reverse the process.

Purifying sugar formed by the hydrolysis of cellulose may never be economical. Thus trees may never be a common source of food but they may well contribute to our motor fuel supply. Wood can be produced on vast areas of land not well-suited to conventional food crop production. Many advances are being made toward more efficient wood production through breeding superior trees, shorter rotations with close spacing and the application of other new technology.

No massive fermentation alcohol production scheme can be visualized unless agronomically sound cellulose, sugar or starch production can be established in the currently little-developed wet tropics, for example in the Amazon Valley. Only in such areas are temperatures and rainfall favorable for the year-round capture of the sun's energy through the use of green plants. Many problems of tropical soil management to insure perpetual fertility would have to be overcome, but it might be possible with efficient crops such as sugar cane, napier grass, cassava or one of the many rapidly growing woody species.

There is another approach to producing energy from the products of the land that is technically feasible and under some circumstances may be economically sound. Most organic materials, provided with the right mineral additives, can be fermented under anaerobic conditions (in the absence of air) to produce methane, the major component of the natural gas you use at home. Currently a large feedlot in Colorado is building a plant to convert their mountains of manure to methane to be used largely in their own farming and packing plant operations. Tractors and trucks can be adapted to operate on methane and of course it may be used for heating in the same ways as natural gas is now employed. Even though a few farmers are reported to be operating their own methane generators, it seems more likely that such a venture would succeed on a co-operative basis. Such "by-product" energy from methane would hardly go far in supplying the vast needs of intensive cropping areas but its production would seem to tie in well with animal agriculture. The residue following anaerobic fermentation has fertilizer value similar to the sludge from sewerage disposal plants. Research is also under way on the direct chemical conversion of wastes or fresh plant material to oil and gas. Involved are processes known to chemical engineers as liquefaction, hydrogasification and pyrolysis.

To raise large volumes of plant material for direct use in methane fermenters or for other processes would require land, just as land was needed for raising feed for horses before the days of the tractor and truck. Again one would have to turn to the wet tropics to find large areas of land not now being used for food production and adapted to a year-round yield of huge tonnages of plant material. It is unlikely that agriculture can ever become self-sufficient in energy but there are many opportunities for it to make valuable contributions. I am convinced that as our fossil fuels are being depleted we should be devoting more effort to learning how best to capture solar energy through the most efficient species of plants grown to give optimum yields.

If we think about the long-range consequences of our dwindling fuel supply, many changes in lifestyle can be visualized such as greatly reduced use of the motorcar, smaller homes and a shift to apartments, and less use of fuel and electric power for heating and cooling. But what of our food? Will we have to rely more on crops and livestock grown locally with less energy expended on transportation? Will energy-demanding processed foods become less plentiful and packaging designed more for conservation than for convenience? Animal products have a high energy requirement because they represent "concentrated" forage and grain which in themselves require much energy for their production. Will we have fewer of these products in our diet of the future?

Some would say that the long-range answer is yes to all those questions. I would qualify the reply. Much depends on progress in the development of new sources of energy but much also depends on how people respond to the better understanding we now have of future food problems. If sensible diets and food conservation prevail together with a continuing slowdown in population growth, our food may not have to be greatly different at the turn of the century or later than it is at this time. If new sources of energy are slow in coming and the petroleum crisis deepens, then allocation to insure our food supply may come sooner than we would like to think. If this had to be a permanent thing because new sources of energy were not in sight, our present luxury diet would most certainly change.

It is important in looking for places to conserve energy and at the possible need for fuel allocation to understand what our present energy budget looks like. Various activities leading to food on the table are estimated to consume 12 to 15 percent of all energy utilized in the United States. A recent task force of the Council for Agricultural Science and Technology broke down this total food energy budget as follows:

Function	Percent of Total
Agricultural Production	18
Food Processing and Packaging	33
Food Transportation	3
Wholesale and Retail Distribution	16
Household and Institutional preparation and refrigeration	30
	100

No doubt other estimates will vary from the above by a few percentage points but regardless they do indicate a few facts. Even a phenomenal reduction in the energy expended between planting a crop and serving your dinner could have but a modest impact on the total energy consumed. Obviously, a significant reduction in the energy needed to put food on your table will require savings in processing, distribution and even in your kitchen. You rural dwellers, think how few days of the year you see farm equipment operating. Then reflect on the fact that your stove is in daily use and your refrigerator requires energy to keep it cold almost hourly.

Many agriculturists are striving to reduce the energy required to produce food and at present costs they have a real incentive. Much less tillage is being practiced by many farmers and some have learned how to raise crops without disturbing the soil at all, thus saving valuable tractor fuel. The energy savings that producers are attempting to achieve, although important, can have no more than a small effect on the overall energy budget. Let's look at some statistics that will bring in focus the modest energy needs of the farmer in relation to the rest of the economy. In spite of much being written about the huge supplies of natural gas utilized for the manufacture of nitrogen fertilizer, it amounts to less than two percent of all gas consumed. The per capita utilization of nitrogen fertilizer for food production purposes has the energy equivalent of less than a tank full of gasoline. Combined farm energy needs including that used to manufacture tractors, fertilizer and other inputs add up to no more than three percent of the total energy consumed in the United States. Of course, any reduction is important but let's not expect farmers to make savings that would lessen the need for conservation in every segment of the economy.

Many years ago it was established that diminishing returns are realized on increased fertilizer use. Above a certain level depending on the crop and soil involved, the application of another increment of fertilizer may not give the farmer a good return on his added investment. As fertilizer requires energy to produce and deliver to the farm so here too there is a point beyond which additional fertilization would be wasteful. At present fertilizer prices, I doubt that many fields are being overfertilized. Certainly the food return per unit of energy expended in farming can never be favorable if crops are poorly nourished or poorly protected from weeds, insects and diseases. As much energy is needed for preparation of soil and planting of a poor crop as for a productive one.

Much research aimed at more productive agriculture is also aimed at the greatest food return per unit of energy. Higher yielding or disease-resistant varieties, better systems of pest control and reduced losses in storage cannot help but make our energy devoted to farming go further. Recent research on modified tillage methods is already reducing the amount of tractor fuel needed for field operations. More efficient natural nitrogen fixation and efficient use of solar energy for crop drying are needs that should be getting more research attention. And let's not forget those vast energy inputs between the farm and your shopping basket. Research on energy saving methods of packaging, storage and distribution should not be overlooked.

There is little risk of wind erosion following fall plowing on many soils but others including the one pictured here can blow readily, resulting in clogged ditches and an increase in the silting of streams. Avoiding fall tillage of such soils is recommended. Stubble mulch tillage is another approach to minimizing blowing soil.

11

My Crystal Ball

Now that we have looked at the past and the present of agriculture and our food supply, what of the future? Will supermarket shelves be full 10 or 20 years hence when most of us will still be eating, I hope as regularly as now. What of the 21st century when my generation which has seen the recent agricultural revolutions unfold will no longer be here. Will you younger readers see still further changes that can insure bountiful harvests for a population that will inevitably continue to grow for a considerable period even if our most optimistic birth control projections come true? Or will society, seeking a Utopian world of zero risks to health and an idealistic environment, outsmart itself and create the greatest health and environmental hazard of all, a shortage of food.

It is a temptation to omit predictions regarding future food supply and the problems we are going to face. The road of the prophets is strewn with miscalculations. It is easier to find failures than successes in the agricultural forecasting business. Who would have guessed a generation ago that we would have doubled our average yield of crops in North America? But then, who would have predicted the tremendous demand from abroad during recent years that has taken up this remarkable increase in productivity? You will recall that Malthus held a dim view of man's future nearly two centuries ago when the population of the world was less than one-third what it is today. He could not foresee the vast improvements in agricultural productivity made possible through the development of new lands particularly in the Americas, not to mention the more recent advances in technology. Perhaps Joseph was the most perceptive crop forecaster of all with his seven fat years and seven lean years.

I'll not attempt to tell you what your steak will cost a decade from now or whether there will be steak available every day, nor will I be so specific as the Paddock brothers who chose *Famine 1975* as a title for their book. But I will risk forecasting some trends and problems we are going to face at some time in the future. Whether it is one year or the next or even one decade or the next is not too significant. The important thing is to understand what is coming and do some sound thinking about it in advance. In this way some problems can be avoided and others stand a better chance of a solution when they do occur.

Food supply depends on the extent of plantings and the numbers of animals being cared for on the one hand, and the unit productivity of these enterprises on the other. Let's look at these factors for the more technically advanced and agriculturally prosperous countries. Economists estimate that for the United States just to cover population growth and probable increased demand while maintaining present high exports would require a food production increase of over two percent per year. Support for the greater export demand that some anticipate during the next few years would require an additional annual increase of two percent. Much depends, of course, on the state of the world's economy. Only a portion of such increases can come from improved efficiency, making some expansion in acreage necessary.

A crucial question in the mind of the farmer considering increased production are the prices he expects to receive. Farming expansion takes time, particularly for livestock and fruit. No one seems to be able to project what will happen to prices during the next decade and many farmers are taking a wait-and-see attitude before undertaking expansion. It was difficult for consumers to recognize that the few cents per pound reduction in 1974 meat prices at the supermarket compared with a year earlier reflected a marked reduction in the return to the farmer for his livestock. Considering the high cost of feed and other inputs, the livestock farmer is in a severe economic squeeze at this writing in early 1975. Because of the ever-mounting cost of conversion of live animals to products ready for you to drop in your shopping basket, the grower's significantly reduced selling price has a seemingly insignificant effect on your food budget. Grain producers with good yields are doing well financially but they are also looking at the economic plight of the livestock producer. They are fully aware of the rapid drop in livestock prices in a few short months following their peak in 1973. Might the same thing happen to wheat, corn and soybeans?

As a consumer, you would like to see an all-out increase in production but you should understand why many a farmer-businessman may go slow on expansion. At high interest rates, an additional tractor and equipment to match could be disastrous if prices again drop too low. In the words of Agricultural Economists L. R. Kyle and G. L. Johnson of Michigan State University: "Neither next year's future prices nor current short-term and long-term governmental forecasts indicate that present prices are expected to persist for the next decade; however, experience in the months and years to come may give farmers firmer price expectations. Price boycotts, price ceilings, and similar actions tend to signal to producers that consumers and/or the government feel higher prices are not warranted. It will be very difficult to gear for substantially greater production unless the more favorable prices are expected to last for several years. Controls to reduce prices would entail rationing because consumers would want to consume more than would be supplied."

I will add that to institute export controls just to create a domestic surplus and keep prices down would most certainly discourage farmers from expansion, which is a sure way to even greater scarcity. We must be certain that any limitations placed on the export of basic farm commodities is really needed to insure an adequate domestic supply. At one extreme, a "no holds barred" export policy could sometimes result in shortages at home while at the other, export controls designed to keep prices down would stifle incentive and result in lower farm productivity. There must be flexibility and compromise on this delicate issue.

A key to expansion in agricultural production is the farmer's guess as to his future cost increases. Farm equipment, tractor fuel, fertilizer and feed have increased at a terrific rate. Many a farmer will go slow on expansion until it appears certain that essential supplies will be available at a cost he can pay and still make a profit at the prices he anticipates for his produce. Major restraints to expanded production at this writing are very tight credit and exceedingly high interest rates. Aside from other factors, expansion in food production will be held back until financing is more readily available.

So acres planted and livestock raised may not go up as rapidly as one might assume considering recent prices. How about crop yield and livestock productivity? Given reasonably good weather I believe yields will edge up further particularly with crops that have not increased rapidly in the past. But we can't expect another 25 years of phenomenal increases like the last. Many growers are going to find it difficult and sometimes costly to increase yields further. The hope is that the marginal farmer who has not yet participated to the fullest extent in the yield revolution will increase his productivity and thus improve the average. New technology will no doubt help but remember that much of this is needed just to hold our own. It takes a constant flow of new disease resistant varieties to balance the capability of fungi to mutate to more virulent strains. New pest problems arise requiring research aimed at a solution and much current effort is being directed toward ecologically safer programs. Yes, there will be improvements in production efficiency as the result of research and development efforts but probably not many phenomenal breakthroughs such as hybrid corn or synthetic nitrogen fertilizer.

So with acreage and livestock increases being far from assured and with weather variables being what they always are, food supplies and therefore prices are likely to vary more than in the past two decades. Remember we had huge grain surpluses in storage during the 1950s and 1960s so occasional reduced yields due to adverse weather had little effect on commodity prices. Now, without much of a reserve, just the threat of a drought sends the futures' market skyrocketing. You will not go hungry but there will be shortages of some things at some times, a situation the affluent world is going to have to learn to live with. The sugar situation of late 1974 gave us a sampling.

We can be certain, however, that people abroad will continue to want North American farm products. In recent years, much has been given outright to alleviate famine and many forecasters believe that even greater famines are in store for countries without food reserves. The lean years and fat years have always been with us and there is no reason to think weather patterns and cycles will change. Will we again provide free grain or sell it for soft currencies if we lack large surpluses such as existed when most of our food relief and Food for Freedom programs were in operation? If we follow the Paddock brothers' recommendation we will be very selective in famine relief programs, confining aid to those countries who have demonstrated a capability of solving their population and agricultural problems but who are temporarily in need. Others they would have us forget. What will we do if this question of charity for the most needy arises when other countries with hard cash are knocking on our door wanting to buy all the food we can spare? In a question of selling versus giving away when one's balance of payments is already in a sorry state, the answer is pretty obvious.

So far these are the easy questions. What if there is strong demand from hard currency countries but our own food reserves are approaching a risky level? Do we continue to export so we can import oil, coffee and radios and travel freely abroad? I, for one, think we need several months reserve of wheat, soybeans and feed grains, hopefully without the necessity of export restrictions. But if a real crunch comes no country is justified in exporting itself into a food crisis. Export controls on foodstuffs might have to be matched by gasoline rationing since oil-rich countries might demand grain rather than dollars. I will still vote for a healthy grain reserve. I am hopeful that an emergency reserve for bread grains can be established soon, one that will be outside the world trade economy as suggested in chapter 4.

Is our climate changing as some weather people seem to think? Unusually dry weather in some parts of the world and excessive rains in others together with a slight cooling trend may herald a period of lower mean temperatures than experienced in recent years. The late spring and early frosts in much of North America in 1974 lend support to the concept of a changing climate. If we can no longer raise corn and soybeans as far north as Minnesota and the Dakotas, the crops now common in Canada may have to be substituted. They include wheat for bread, barley for livestock feed and sunflower and rapeseed for cooking oil. The northern limits of profitable farming in Canada might move south. Agriculture can adapt but food productivity per unit area cannot be so great with a short growing season.

Dry spells within a given year and also longer range drought cycles have been with us since before the invention of agriculture. Now that we can provide plants with the nutrients they need and protect crops against the onslaught of most insects and diseases, the lack of adequate water in the soil is the most likely limiting factor in productivity. There are, no doubt, opportunities for impounding more of the excess water of winter and spring to provide for irrigation during critical dry periods of summer, but we will still be highly dependent on good rainfall distribution. Much of the lower yields of corn and soybeans in 1974 resulted from a relatively short spell of very hot and dry weather following a wet spring. Late summer rains came too late to insure a good crop in many sections of the midwestern United States. Rainfall for the year was not particularly low but unfavorable distribution was a disaster for many growers and prevented building the food reserves that could have helped keep possible future inflation in check.

How about the kinds of food we will have in abundance in the future? Are there new ones in the offing? Are some likely to be in short supply and others more plentiful? Even now in the affluent developed countries economics may be dictating a somewhat lower per capita consumption of animal products and it seems unlikely that the long-term climb in meat consumption will continue. Pigs and chickens are really only grain and oilseed meal converters and unless we find ways to lower costs and increase productivity of these commodities, poultry meat and particularly pork consumption will be restricted by price. As discussed earlier, beef can be produced on forage with little or no input of grain, but the low reproductive efficiency of the beef animal together with the high cost of land, fertilizer and fencing will inevitably keep prices high.

There are opportunities for vast increases in grass-fed beef production in many parts of the world but with even a modest increase in buying power the demand will go up, possibly faster than supplies can increase. Almost everyone likes beef and will spend a part of any increase in income on this meat. I expect more people to be eating some beef but many middle income families in the developed countries may have a little less. Much depends on the economy and how fast that can change! Certainly the 100 million people in the Arab countries should now be able to afford more meat.

What will be the effect on beef quality of current trends toward more grass feeding with shorter finishing periods on grain? On the average your beef will probably be leaner and possibly not as tender as you like, but I am confident it will be quite acceptable. I doubt that the practice of finishing cattle is on the way out even though high grain prices have discouraged long periods in the feedlot. There will always be off-grade grain not suitable for human food. Cattle feeders are using more high-yielding corn silage to produce good beef at favorable costs, even though growth rates are somewhat slower than with more concentrated feed. Considering the beef animal's ability to utilize nonprotein nitrogen and forage from land not suited to cropping, together with the fact that it can be finished for superior quality largely on silage, the bovine species has many ecological and economic assets to balance its inefficiencies.

Among the cereals, rice is likely to increase its share of total food consumption. Already 60 percent of the world's people get a large portion of their calories from rice and this is likely to increase. Much of the world's acreage adapted to wheat and other temperate zone cereals is already in cultivation but there is much land in warmer climates that can be successfully developed for rice. True, much progress has been made in breeding wheat adapted to warmer climates, but considering the soil factor I see vastly greater opportunities for increased rice production. With the right seed and other inputs together with the best cultural methods, rice has a high yield potential and only a modest part of the globe's quarter billion acres of this crop has had the benefit of modern technology. Between increased yields and increased land devoted to rice, world production can be stepped up more than for any other food crop. Coming from a potato country, I will order the spud for most of my meals. But considering availability and economy, millions will be eating more rice, and since this is a low protein crop, more legumes or animal products will be needed for balanced nutrition.

Processed foods have become so common in our time there seems to be little resistance to the acceptance of something new. The idea of meat extenders and substitutes made directly from cereals or legumes may not appeal to you but I predict more of them will appear on the market and be widely used. Economics will be on their side. In several less developed countries, much effort has gone into various types of "synthetic" milk-like products which derive their protein largely from plant sources. These have been only moderately successful and at the present high price of once cheap soybean meal and other plant protein, it isn't clear that they have much of an economic advantage over a dairy operation based on well-managed pastures, particularly if the protein for the synthetic product has to be imported. I believe that at least in temperate zone countries the conversion of forage to milk will continue to be one of our more efficient ways in which to obtain protein for human nutrition. Whether used fresh, dried for low cost transport and distribution or converted to cheese, milk is an efficient way to obtain human food from land ill-suited to the raising of food crops.

As critical as production efficiency is to The Food in Your Future good storage is equally important. In addition to the huge terminal grain silos often seen by travelers, farm storage adequate to prevent losses from mold, insects and rodents is becoming more common. Here dry grain is being held in metal structures on a midwestern farm.

12

You-A Part of the Solution?

Along with thousands of other agricultural specialists I hope to contribute to a continuing flow of new technology that will help insure an abundance of food at your shopping center in future years. Given a reasonable level of incentive I know that crop and livestock producers as well as their suppliers and those who process, store and ship farm products will strive to make their enterprises productive and efficient. But we can't assure future generations adequate food all by ourselves. You, Mr. and Mrs. Johnny Q. Citizen, also have a responsibility for future food supply and what's more you can do something about it. You can be a part of the solution rather than a part of the problem. Here's how.

1. Contribute to population control. Every increase in population means a need for more food. The slowing birthrates in many parts of the world are encouraging but they must continue. I believe we can vastly increase agricultural production but a look at the simple arithmetic of population growth makes

it very clear that our finite land resources are no match for man's infinite capacity to reproduce. Somewhere along the line population growth must cease if we are to be adequately fed and I think that in most parts of the globe the sooner this happens the better.

2. Adopt a sensible diet. Obviously food consumption in excess of nutritional need adds to total demand and can contribute to shortages. As pointed out earlier, animal products require many times the agricultural, financial and energy resources as food derived from plants. Protein from meat, milk and eggs is healthful and provides the simplest way to insure a balanced diet. But to consume large excesses of protein over that required for good nutrition as most people in the wealthier countries do today just doesn't make sense for the future. Eating meat a little less often with more modest servings will not only be good for your pocketbook but help reverse a dietary trend which if continued could contribute to severe food shortages at some time in the future. Perhaps the housewife who learns how to prepare more interesting meals with less meat is doing something worthwhile for posterity as well as the financial well-being of her own family. Not the least of the benefits would be the easing of inflationary pressures of a tight grain supply.

3. Extend your moderation to the nonfood demands you place on agricultural resources. Remember that beer, liquors and wine are all derived from the land, starting out as grain or fruit. Tea, coffee and soft drinks as well as tobacco get their start on farms some place in the world. Sensible diets for pets can ease demands on food resources. Excessively high protein rations are no more essential for healthy dogs and cats than they are for people. Horses can thrive on a diet high in roughages and low in grain.

4. Don't be alarmed at temporary shortages. We've grown so used to having perishables every day of the year that we sometimes forget they must be grown and harvested in

different areas at various seasons and the weather is often unco-operative. If there is a shortage of lettuce in the fall after the summer crop is finished and before the winter crop in the Imperial Valley is ready, just be patient and eat cole slaw for a couple of weeks. If a stored crop is near exhaustion before the new harvest, as was the case with raisins in the summer of 1973, it's hardly fair to buy all the packages you can find and hoard them. The new crop will be available soon and after all, you can get along without raisins for a while. Quantity buying in the interests of economy and shopping convenience makes a lot of sense but unusual stocking up of an item just because it is temporarily short is out-and-out hoarding and not very good citizenship. Hoarding will only hasten the need for rationing and nothing gives government so much control over our lives. The day of Orwell's Big Brother may be closer than we think if food hoarding ever brings on the need for food rationing as a permanent institution.

5. Don't join the Hunger Mongers. Recognize the need to preserve our better lands for agricultural use and support zoning laws accordingly. Garden organically if you like; it's an interesting hobby. But recognize that you are largely moving plant nutrients from one soil to another and for real farmers to produce the colossal tonnages of food needed for the billions of people in the world, the minerals that plants need for good growth must be supplied from other sources. Also, remember that once the mineral supply of a soil is properly adjusted the bigger crops produced leave larger organic residues in the soil. Today's good farmer is returning more organic matter to his fields than ever before.

6. By all means, recognize that crops and livestock must be protected from a myriad of insects, diseases, nematodes, viruses, weeds, and other pests if the world is to eat. Much has been and will continue to be accomplished by

genetic and biological methods. But these must be integrated with chemical control. At the present time there is no other way if your grandchildren are to avoid hunger. Learn about the intricate regulations we now have which assure human and environmental safety. Of course, even the newer and safer pesticides offer some risk if grossly misused, but to block their availability even though properly applied is to contribute to a less productive agriculture and lead to the greatest health and ecological risk of all, a shortage of food.

7. Encourage sensible regulations. Legislators and control officials are indeed very responsive to public opinion and they are being constantly hounded by the Hunger Mongers to eliminate or greatly restrict the use of crop and livestock protection chemicals. Various pressure groups are continually urging regulations that would greatly restrict the productivity of agriculture. Obviously, regulations are needed. But if the overregulation and the absolutely no-risk philosophy that some promote continues to prevail, we are going to find ourselves short of food, perhaps in only a very few years. These pressures by the Hunger Mongers can be balanced by expressions of public opinion urging practical controls to give us safety when materials are properly used but at the same time give us the benefits of the crop and livestock protection that is absolutely essential to our future.

8. Recognize that a wide range of inputs are indispensable to modern farming and shortages of these will only discourage production and result in lower yields. If energy shortages prevent manufacturers from producing the things the farmer needs to raise food then allocation will have to be faced up to and tough decisions made. Similar decisions may be needed relative to the energy required for storage, processing and distribution. You should have a part in making them.

9. On a more positive note, support those policies that are needed to insure the further increases in productivity required for an expanding population and also to provide a better diet for those who are now ill-fed. Agricultural research and development supported by public funds has paid off in the past and its future funding is one of our best hedges against shortages. Early in 1974 Senator Lloyd Bentsen, a spokesman for those who recognize the importance of further research to the food in our future, stated in testimony before the U.S. Senate Appropriations Committee:

> Mr. Chairman, at no time in our history has a strong productive agriculture been as important to our Nation's welfare as today. As we project the role that an adequate, hopefully bountiful food supply can play in our country's future, it becomes even more important that we recognize the mammoth task to be undertaken by our agricultural scientists. They must, through their research efforts, help guarantee that our citizens have wholesome and plentiful food available to them, that there will be food available for needed foreign trade, and that likewise we will have food which can be used as a weapon of good will to insure peace in the world. Our scientists need adequate support so that they may accomplish the work that needs to be done.

Industry sponsored research related to agricultural production has also given good returns to investors and has benefited the public. Now what is needed are sensible controls to insure continuing investment in research and development that could help make more food available in the years ahead. Nothing so discourages research investment as the prospect of long delays in obtaining governmental approval for a new crop or livestock protection chemical or other farm supplies.

10. Think through our objectives with respect to the food in our future. There is currently much discussion in the United States of the need for a clear-cut food policy. Jean Mayer, a noted Harvard nutritionist, stated in a syndicated newspaper article late in 1974:

"American food policy should have four aims:
To stimulate food production by American farmers and ensure them a fair return on their labor and investments.
To keep food prices reasonable for American consumers.
To help starving people overseas.
To help even our balance of payments."

I will buy these, but a fifth aim if food production is to keep up with growing needs must be to give a continuing high level of encouragement and financial support to the research and development that can help assure abundant food in our future. Without continuing advances in technology together with the agricultural extension and other educational programs needed to ensure its adoption by farmers, Mayer's four aims will have little chance of achievement in the decades ahead. And of course to be meaningful any food policy must be paralleled with a policy of encouraging birthrates that will keep population in reasonable balance with future resources.

11. Keep abreast of the broad range of pending food and agriculture legislation and express your opinions. In the past there have been a wide range of subsidy schemes to keep farmers solvent and land retirement plans to help alleviate surpluses. Most of these schemes are unnecessary in today's world. Currently the United States has a new law which essentially sets a price floor on major farm crops, the justification being that this will encourage all-out production and thus help keep prices down. Even though floors may be far below current market prices, the law will have a beneficial effect. Without it growers would hesitate to increase production if they thought surpluses might again appear and bankruptcy prices ensue. If exports are restricted, farmers will perceive this as an influence toward lower prices, and a price floor might then be very essential to high productivity.

There are always pressures from some segments of agriculture for high price floors, ones that would take practically all the risk out of farming. We know from past experiences that troublesome surpluses can develop if we go too far in that direction. A floor that absorbs only a part of the risk without nullifying the normal economic forces of supply and demand seems the best way to encourage productivity without risking huge surpluses far in excess of those needed for a prudent reserve.

In the United States the federal government has often sponsored such partially subsidized programs as crop insurance, soil conservation activities and financing for agricultural production. Concessionary credit has often been provided to farmers in areas that have suffered from a natural catastrophe such as a flood or severe drought. Perhaps these have been overdone at times, but if our urban majority in Congress is tempted to wipe out these farm programs they should do so only after careful study of the effect such action might have on food productivity and the price increases that would inevitably follow if smaller crops were produced. Modified farm legislation will be proposed from time to time and as a good citizen you should recognize that the wrong political action could seriously affect your future food supply.

12. Take part in foreign aid decisions. The future of food aid for hungry people in the developing countries depends in part on availability of supplies but much also depends on you. The United States and other technically advanced nations have provided a tremendous amount of aid since World War II. Many programs are still being carried out although on a reduced scale. There is currently much discussion in the world's capitals about the food shortages already here or on the horizon in many parts of the world. A major topic for discussion at the November 1974 World Food Conference in Rome was the establishment of an international food reserve. Such a buffer could be very beneficial in dire emergencies

but a reserve should be hard to get at. Political leaders everywhere must recognize that they have the responsibility to develop their own agriculture and to maintain their own domestic reserve as a first line of defense against hunger. Too many in the past have failed to support the measures that could help their own farmers increase production because they could always fall back on the stored surplus in the United States and other grain growing countries.

President Ford pledged in a 1974 speech to the United Nations that the United States would increase its budget for famine relief programs. He did not mention that with the price increases of farm commodities and transportation in the last few years, a very large budget expansion would be needed to maintain the past level of relief provided by the United States. Later, at the time of the World Food Conference in Rome, the United States found itself unable to pledge a meaningful increase in food relief because of the relatively poor yields of corn and soybeans in 1974. None-the-less, relief shipments on a significant scale are proceeding, particularly to Bangladesh.

Senator Hubert Humphrey has suggested that one less hamburger per week for all Americans would feed tens of millions of people elsewhere through savings in grain. Had he referred to high-grade roasts and steak or to pork or poultry his calculations would be right, but he apparently did not recognize how much hamburger as well as processed meat products such as hotdogs come from old dairy cows, beef brood cows or grass-fed animals. Obviously only a lowering in consumption of fowl or grain-fed animals raised for slaughter can result in a savings in grain. Some reduction in the consumption of meat produced from grain by the affluent may be desirable but it should not be a substitute for improving agricultural productivity in all corners of the earth.

Answers to the food relief question will be easy if major grain growing countries again have a surplus after assuring their own needs and filling purchase orders from countries with hard currencies. But will the affluent nations eat less, will they reduce their intake of grain-fed meat and will they modify their indulgences in nonfood beverages, in pets, in tobacco and in well-fertilized lawns so they can extend a helping hand to food-short people? Just what policy the more affluent countries can or should follow in future years relative to relief programs has yet to be determined. We are in for much soul searching and debate. I am convinced that a better answer will come forth if you participate to the fullest extent possible.

13. Consider various subsidy programs from different viewpoints. Government subsidized irrigation schemes have long been popular in many countries and there are those who argue that the farmer should pay for the true value of the water he uses. No doubt low cost water has sometimes encouraged inefficient use. If new irrigation plans are proposed, as they most certainly will be as population pressures increase, the question of how much of the cost of water should be charged to the price of producing food and how much subsidized by the public needs careful consideration. Some subsidy is often needed to get a project started, but irrigation is, after all, a part of the cost of farming. Should it be passed on to the consumer as a part of the price he pays for food or should he pay for it in the taxes needed to provide a continuing subsidy? You or your legislative representatives will some day have to make this decision.

14. Support land-use planning concepts that take future food needs into consideration. Certainly there must be a limit to how far we can go in providing extra-wide right-of-ways unless utilization of the land involved is a part of the planning. How long can we allow suburbs to

continue their spread onto our best agricultural soils? You can help formulate the answers.

There must also some day be an end to the diversion of good crop or grazing land to recreational or nature preserves. In my view the current pressure by environmentalists to outlaw grazing on public lands in the western United States just doesn't make sense. Of course there have at times been some unwise management practices. But to forgo income from grazing fees and at the same time deprive people of the wool and meat from millions of sheep and cattle as a means of correcting abuses is surely cutting off our nose to spite our face. Grazing lands can be managed to conserve soil and at the same time encourage wildlife and recreational use. If you have convictions on this subject let your representatives in the Congress know how you feel.

15. Raise a garden if you have land available where the cost and time involved in getting to it is not too great. Its contribution in terms of pounds of food may be modest but gardening can be fun. Start out small if you are a beginner. With good fertilization and care it's astonishing how much can be raised in so little space. Better to expand after a small but successful beginning than to get discouraged with too big a project.

16. When you throw food in the garbage think of the land, labor and energy resources needed to produce it. Having always lived in homes where waste was minimal I sometimes cringe at the food I see going to waste as restaurant or banquet dishes are cleared. Better than any preaching I can do is to quote Hank Aaron on an experience in his early days of professional baseball while eating with a fellow player, Jenkins, who had obviously grown up in a home where food was precious. Let Aaron tell it as he did in a recent issue of *Guideposts:*

> Jenkins was a pitcher and I roomed with him when we were traveling. He was tall and bony with big eyes and real short hair.

One night I was about to drink a container of milk when a bug flew into it. Disgusted, I poured it out. Jenkins was watching me.

"Aaron, do you know how many people in this world would have given anything for that milk you poured out?"

"There was a bug in it."

"That doesn't matter. Waste is a sin. There are too many starving people in this world for us to waste food like that."

Perhaps Jenkins is better prepared for the future than most of us in the affluent world.

17. Finally a word to farmers or others who have land under their stewardship. Take it as a sacred trust. You didn't make the land. It is only yours to use for a short span of time but long enough to undo thousands of years of natural soil building processes. If you keep your soil in place and practice all we have learned about fertility improvement, you can then pass it on to its next custodian with the satisfaction of having exercised good stewardship and with the knowledge that it can be more productive of food than when you took it over. Thus you will have made a valuable contribution to the food supply of future generations.

Suggested Additional Reading

Modern Soy Bean Production, Walter O. Scott and Samuel Aldrich, Farm Quarterly, Cincinnati, Ohio, 1970. (Available from the senior author, University of Illinois, Urbana.)

Modern Corn Production, Samuel Aldrich and Earl R. Leng, Farm Quarterly, Cincinnati, Ohio, 1965. (Available from the senior author, University of Illinois, Urbana.)

No-Tillage Farming, S. H. Phillips and H. M. Young Jr., Reiman Associates, Milwaukee, Wisconsin, 1973.

Erosion and Sediment Pollution Control, R. P. Beasley, Iowa State University Press, Ames, Iowa, 19720

A New Look At Energy Sources, Publication No. 22, American Society of Agronomy, Madison, Wisconsin, 1974.

Agricultural Production Efficiency, National Academy of Sciences, Washington, D. C., 1975.

Productive Agriculture — A Quality Environment, National Academy of Sciences, Washington, D. C., 1974.

By Bread Alone, Lester R. Brown with Erik P. Eckholm, Praeger, New York, 1974.

The Food And People Problem, George Borgstrom, Duxbury Press, Belmont, California, 1974.

The Limits Of Growth, Donella Meadows et al., Universe Books, New York, 1972.

The Population Problem, Arthur McCormack, Crowell, New York, 1970.

Famine 1975, William and George Paddock, Little Brown, Boston, 1967.

Ecological Fantasies — Death From Falling Watermelons, A. Adler, Green Eagle Press, New York, 1973.

Food In History, Reay Tannahill, Stein and Day, New York, 1973.

Campaign Against Hunger, E. C. Stakeman et al., Belknap Press of Harvard University Press, Cambridge, Massachusetts, 1967.

Famine On The Wind — Man's Battle Against Plant Disease, G. L. Carefoot and E. R. Sprott, Rand McNally and Company, 1967.

Hunger Fighters, Paul DeKruif, Harcourt Brace, New York, 1928.

The Great Hunger — Ireland 1845-49, C. B. Woodham-Smith, H. Hanulton, London, 1962.

Principles Of Plant And Animal Pest Control, Published by the National Academy of Sciences, Washington, D. C.

Volume 1 (1968)	*Plant Disease Development And Control*
Volume 2 (1968)	*Weed Control*
Volume 3 (1969)	*Insect Pest Management And Control*
Volume 4 (1969)	*The Control Of Plant Parasitic Nematodes*
Volume 5 (1970)	*The Vertebrates That Are Pests: Problems And Control*

Agriculture: Food and Man (a study guide), Robert L. Park, et al., Brigham Young University Press, Provo, Utah, 1975.

Science, 188, No. 4188 (May 9, 1975) (an issue devoted to food problems).

Environmental Benefits of Intensive Crop Production, Keith C. Barrons, Agricultural Science Review, Vol. 9, No. 2, 1971, pp. 33-39.

Why The Food Crisis, Jean Mayer, *Reader's Digest, 106,* No. 637 (May, 1975), pp. 73-77.

Seeds To Civilization — The Story of Man's Food, Charles B. Neiser, W. H. Freeman and Company, San Francisco, 1973.

Index